GINGER KID

KID

Mostly true tales
from a former nerd

AMULET BOOKS
NEW YORK

GINGER KID

mostly true
tales from
a former nerd

Stand-up Comedian and YouTube Personality

STEVE HOFSTETTER

Cataloging-in-Publication Data has been applied for and
may be obtained from the Library of Congress.

ISBN 978-1-4197-2870-9

Text copyright © 2018 Steve Hofstetter
Book design by Alyssa Nassner

Printed and bound in USA
10 9 8 7 6 5 4 3 2 1

Amulet Books are available at special discounts when
purchased in quantity for premiums and promotions as
well as fundraising or educational use. Special editions
can also be created to specification. For details, contact
specialsales@abramsbooks.com or the address below.

ABRAMS The Art of Books
195 Broadway, New York, NY 10007
abramsbooks.com

TO "JACOB," "MASON," "OZZIE,"
"RANDY," AND "REBECCA."

WITHOUT YOU, THIS WOULD
HAVE GONE VERY DIFFERENTLY.

CONT

OPENER, FEATURE, HEADLINER. A TYPICAL AMERICAN comedy show is divided up into those three acts, in that order.

The Opener is so raw and in over their head that, no matter how much promise they may have, they're often completely lost.

The Feature finally has the experience and knowledge to advance past being the opener, but their desperation to become the headliner can lead to failure.

The Headliner, however, takes the failures they've lived through during their earlier stages and uses those lessons to develop the quiet confidence that comes from finally understanding the game.

That, in essence, describes my high school journey.

Opener, Feature, Headliner.

OPENER

CONT

FEATURE

HEADLINER

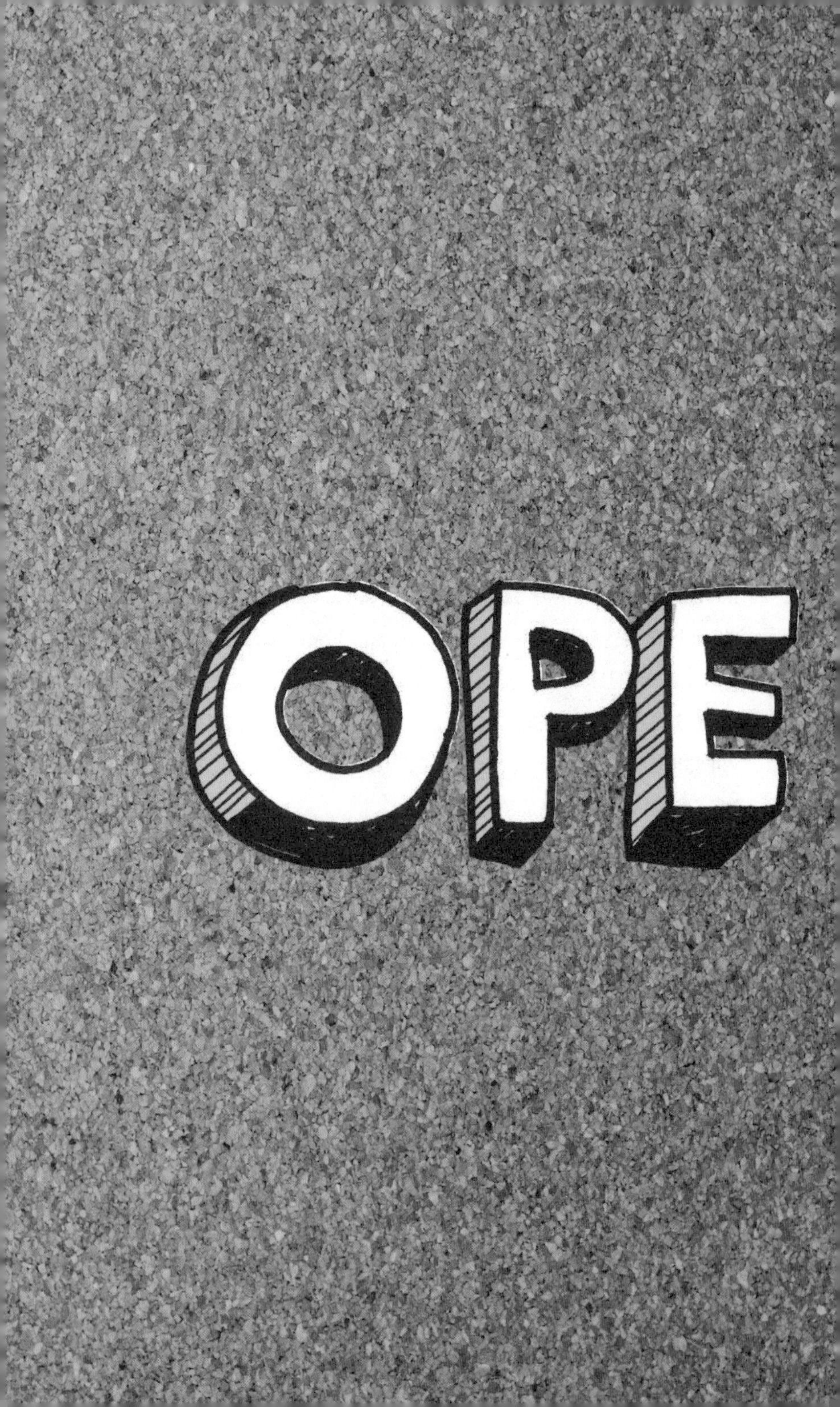
OPE

ONE QUICK THING

HI. MAYBE YOU'RE READING THIS BECAUSE YOU HAVE good taste in books; or someone you know has good taste in books; or someone who threw this out used to have good taste in books, before they became a jerk. No matter the reason, hi.

I don't know exactly why you're reading this book, but I know exactly why I'm writing it. I've gotten to do some pretty cool things in my life. I'm a stand-up comedian, and I perform a few hundred shows a year. More than one hundred million people have watched me on YouTube. I've been in some movies and even hosted my own TV show. And I'm writing this while on a plane to New Zealand. Don't worry—I didn't just mail myself there. I'm actually going for a show. Life has been good.

But if you had predicted any of this when I was in high school, I wouldn't have believed you. Partially because I'd have been wary of the sorcery you used to glimpse the future. But mainly because for me, life in high school was *not* good. I was a scared, shy redhead from Queens who spent way more time getting made fun of than being funny. The only way I'd have believed I was going to New Zealand by myself is if one of the bullies mailed me there.

As I got older, I learned that most of us get bullied. Most of us get scared. And most of us have never been to New Zealand by ourselves. Except people from New Zealand; they've pretty much all been there at some point. I hear it's super-nice. Maybe I'll let you know in the next book.

The exact reason I'm writing this book is because I wanted to share my story in the hope that you can see it as your own. Spoiler alert: My story comes out okay in the end. I'm hoping that yours does, too.

OLD SCHOOL AND NEW SCHOOL

I WAS A PRETTY HAPPY KID. AND THEN, I WASN'T.

Baseball is not an easy sport to play one-on-one, but my brother, David, and I improvised. We would walk the block to our schoolyard, and one of us would play outfield while the other hit fly balls. Our lives would probably have been easier if we preferred basketball. But we wanted to be baseball players, so we played baseball.

Meanwhile, my sister Beth and I would spend most nights dreaming up crazy stories about what our future lives would look like. Sometimes she was a doctor and I was a lawyer. More often, I was a baseball player and she was an actress. Every time, we were both rich and not living in a three-bedroom house with six people. And, every time, we would laugh.

But I was at my happiest when I was in school.

I know that sounds strange. What normal kid is happy in school? Don't misunderstand: I looked forward to dismissal and the weekend and summer vacation like everyone else. But when I was a kid, school was good to me. Because school was easy.

The first thing that made school easy was the familiarity. I'm the youngest of four and from Briarwood, a neighborhood in Queens where teachers work at the same school so long, it's like they're serving time.

I imagine a judge pounding a gavel in front of a roomful of graying, chalk-covered middle-agers. "You are hereby sentenced to twenty-five years of glitter-covered hand turkeys," he'd shout, jowls trembling. The teachers would then shuffle back to their respective faculty lounges, where they'd be met with a lifetime supply of instant coffee and rexo sheets and debate whether or not this was better than picking up trash off a highway.

All my teachers had taught three Hofstetters before me, so I often started the school year being given some sort of in-front-of-the-class responsibility like passing out reading materials or helping pronounce students' names. I accepted with an artificial air of reluctance, thereby not losing my street cred while simultaneously exuding authority.

Meanwhile, my sister Beth was just one year older than I. So when I was in fifth grade, I knew the sixth graders and they knew me. That cemented my street cred. There is no greater grade school validation than an older kid saying hello to you in the hallway and meaning it.

Something important to know about where I grew up is that

Queens is the most diverse county in the country, and Briarwood is the most diverse neighborhood in Queens. There were always twenty to thirty kids who would start the year unable to speak more than a few sentences of English. My closest friends' names were Anant, Jung-Hoon, and Chao. We were a real-life Disney Channel show, except we never formed a band.

Because of the number of students who didn't speak English, school was easy academically. I had an unfair advantage when it came to homework: The school taught toward the students having the most trouble, so those of us who could speak English natively were rarely pushed. The most academically challenging thing we had to do was trace our hands to draw a turkey.

To make school even easier, my siblings were older, and they judged me according to their contemporaries. Sure, some of their classmates were idiots—a boy in Beth's class once interrupted the sex ed presentation to announce he'd do whatever he could to avoid getting his period—but my siblings were smart and their friends were smart, and they demanded the same of me. I was already learning long division in the second grade because David would think I was an idiot if I didn't.

The first time I understood my advantages, I was eleven years old. One of the new teacher's aides was being led around the class by a student named Pampas (really, there were very few kids named Mike or Sarah anywhere near that school), and Pampas stopped when she got to my desk.

"This is Steve," Pampas said. "He's the smartest kid in the school." Because Pampas was named for a heavily populated region in South America, I trusted her opinion.

Kidding. I initially reacted with incredulity. There were hundreds of other students. There had to be someone in this school smarter than I was. I looked around the room and saw most of my classmates giggling at the teacher having "aides." Okay. So maybe I was overestimating my contemporaries.

Before Pampas's declaration, I'd never held myself up against my classmates. I knew I'd always gotten good grades on my report cards, and I aced the citywide math and reading tests. I also drew a solid hand turkey—but who didn't?

When you're a kid, you tend to think what's normal for you is normal for everyone. I never realized my family didn't have money until I babysat for a doctor. Talk about rich! Every one of his kitchen drawers opened without needing to be coaxed with a jiggle. Every. Single. One. That guy was loaded.

Until Pampas said something, I just assumed school was easy because the work was easy—not because I was particularly good at it. But after I considered the possibility that she was right, I started reveling in my new identity. I didn't have to just be the "youngest Hofstetter"—I could have my own thing. I could be the smart kid. Yeah—I liked that.

When the entrance test for Hunter College High School came around, I was excited. Hunter is a competitive public high school in Manhattan. The top 2 percent of students in New York City are selected to take the entrance exam, based on scores from a citywide test you take when you're ten. Then, those in the top 5 percent of scorers on the entrance exam are offered admission to Hunter.

I was one of a handful of students in my school eligible to take the test. The importance of this was not lost on me. This was my big break, and I leaned into my smart-kid persona. For the first time in my life, I studied. I read quiz books. I took practice exams. Anant and I even went to extra math classes taught during lunch. And when the Hunter test came, I was ready.

Unfortunately, Anant was not. Anant was no academic slouch. But while he would go on to attend the University of Pennsylvania, he just missed the cut for Hunter. I was in, but I was in by myself.

It was a big deal for a kid from Briarwood to get into Hunter— it had been years since any of us had been accepted. It was an odd neighborhood; I remember one nasty snowstorm where plows left enormous drifts throughout the neighborhood. I watched two kids play on top of my oldest sister Leah's car for half an hour before realizing it was a car and not just a mound of snow. It took thirty minutes for these kids to deduce that mounds of snow don't usually have visible antennae and windshields and aren't usually in a parking space in between two other cars.

I knew I would miss my friends, but I was excited about being surrounded by other smart kids. What I didn't realize is that I was a sea turtle excited about swimming with sharks.

"Look at their beauty!" My naïve turtle self would exalt, before realizing one of the sharks had just eaten my flipper.

I decided that to fit in at Hunter, I would need to make a good impression, and quickly. Perhaps I wasn't smart after all.

I would have been much better biding my time and finding my friends naturally. Surely there'd be other wannabe baseball players in the school or other people who loved to write. Instead of relying on commonalities, I went with the time-honored approach of coming off as extremely desperate for attention.

My need for attention actually worked in the beginning. At the end of the first day of class, my social studies teacher was going around the room taking attendance. Like every teacher we'd had that day, she asked each of the students what they'd prefer to be called. Kristopher became Kris. Jonathan didn't want to be Jon, and Jennifer transformed to Jenny. I found the pageantry of it all amusing, since no one in Briarwood had ever asked Pampas if she preferred Pam.

When the teacher got to my name, she just called, "Steven," and quickly moved on to the next name without asking me what I preferred. I saw the opportunity for comedy. "Steve, please," I said in an imperious tone, despite never being called Steve by anyone ever. My classmates had already heard me answer to Steven five times that day, and they knew that I was just messing with this one teacher, who looked perplexed as giggles filled the room. I'd taken a shot at the expense of a teacher and it worked. Flaunting authority? *Man, this new kid has guts!*

It was a solid first day of school. And I wish I could have ended on that joke: "Goodnight, everybody! Thank you for coming to high school! I'll see you next year. Remember to tip your waitstaff!" But "Steve, please" was the last joke that landed for an absurdly long time. Like, years. Unfortunately, as the jokes fell flat, I tried harder. The amount of effort was noticeable, and trying too hard is the high school equivalent of putting your Tinder profile on your front door—depressing, pathetic, universally frowned upon, and good at keeping teenagers away from you. My classmates' opinions of me dwindled so quickly that if someone were to graph my popularity from the first day of school to winter break, it would have looked like a black diamond ski slope. Or perhaps a vertical line.

Meanwhile, my teachers got progressively more annoyed. The positive attention I had handed to me from Briarwood faculty was missing at Hunter. These teachers had never seen my family draw hand turkeys. To them, Hofstetter was just the last name of the pretentious kid who insisted on being called Steve.

And as I flailed for social acceptance, I wasn't even the smart kid anymore. That identity had been stripped from me as soon as I got my first real exam back. There was a big red D on the top of the page, and beneath it, a note said, "Steve—you need to try harder." Well, at least she was calling me Steve and not Steven. Small victories.

‹ ‹ ‹

If I'd had an exam to measure my social skills, it would have had a big D at the top with a note that said, "Stop trying so hard." With every terrible joke I made, I flailed more. I was in social quicksand. I went from the new kid who was surprisingly funny to the new kid who wouldn't shut the hell up. So, after weeks of trying and more trying, I did the only thing I could think of to stop the bleeding: I shut the hell up. I stopped raising my hand in class. I stopped talking to strangers in the halls. I stopped being a happy kid.

The fearless red-headed kid who was willing to crack a joke at a teacher's expense on the first day in a new school was gone. Suddenly I was quiet and shy. And I regretted ever leaving Briarwood. I'd have given anything to return to my simple life and run around in the snow on top of a car.

I pictured my neighborhood friends having fun without me. "This is Anant," I envisioned Pampas saying to their new teacher. "He's the smartest kid in the class. Steve was, but he's dead now. Socially, anyway."

The only way to learn how to handle trauma is to experience it. If you grow up in Southern California and you go to college in Minnesota, that first cold winter is really going to sting. That's what Hunter had become for me: endless social tundra with the wind of other students' taunts whipping at my face. I had to learn how to deal with the cold.

At Hunter, I was on my own. And I wasn't happy.

TOMMY
AND THEO

THROUGHOUT MY LIFE, I HAVE FOUND MOST BULLIES TO be painfully uncreative. Every now and then, you get a Shakespeare with fists, but take a look at some YouTube comments and you'll see that a bully's insults typically come in two varieties. The first is a string of obscene-ish words that make no sense together, such as, "You anus boner butt plug." *Um, what*? When someone like that insults you, wear it as a badge of honor. I don't want to be liked by anyone who thinks that "sentence" is worth saying.

The second, more common type of uncreative bully insult is repeated use of the same word until it has absolutely no meaning. The specific words bullies rely on change over time, but the pattern is the same. I have been called a cuck thousands of times in the last year, and every one of those people thought they were being clever. Every one of them was wrong.

In the ninth grade, Tommy Tillet thought he was clever, too. He was also wrong.

I do not know what I did to make Tommy choose me as a target. Perhaps he was jealous of the attention I got from my awesome "Steve, please" line. More likely he did it because he knew I wouldn't fight back.

One of Tommy's favorite go-tos was to loudly interrupt me every time he heard me speaking. This was particularly obnoxious behavior, considering how seldom I spoke. Tommy's interruptions made me want to speak even less often; but being quiet wasn't enough to shield me from Tommy's wrath.

When I'd sit silently, Tommy would stick notes to my back. The notes would say things like STUPID and MORON and other words that in a just world might have been used to describe Tommy himself. Perhaps he was just signing his work.

Tommy relied mainly on pranks you could find in old Archie comics, so at least I knew what was coming.

Theo Webster, however, was a different story.

Theo reveled in making me actually fear for my safety, constantly hinting that at any moment, he would beat me to a pulp. Theo would fake punch me in the hallway to see if I'd flinch, which I did every time. I'd flinch, and he and his goon friends would laugh as if to say, "Look at this loser. Being born with basic protective instincts. What a coward!"

Instilling fear is the most insidious form of bullying, because it makes the target's own mind turn against itself.

"You should probably look over your shoulder more," Theo would say, while his goon friends cackled just over his shoulder.

Then he'd throw half a punch toward my face to see if I'd flinch. And I would.

I imagined elaborate worst-case scenarios. One day, I'd be scared that Theo would shove me down the stairs. The next, that he'd jump me from behind. The next, that he'd stuff me in my locker. This was ridiculous, as the lockers at Hunter are about two feet tall and eight inches wide. Even a car compacter could not stuff me in my locker.

But I was scared. Every day I was scared. Had I already been beaten up in my life, I wouldn't have been as scared. Getting punched, while not desirable, isn't nearly as bad as the fear of getting punched. This is a lesson I unfortunately had to learn later in life. But walking through the hallways, terrified of what may or may not happen—well, I'd rather have been punched.

Not only was I scared of whatever getting beaten up may or may not feel like, but I also started being scared of being scared. I didn't want to be a coward. Would I be like this the rest of my life?

I wanted to stand up for myself. I wanted to tell Tommy that no one thought his notes were funny. I wanted to tell Theo that if he hit me, my older brother would find a way to fit *him* into one of those lockers. But I couldn't. Partially because I didn't have the courage, and partially because I'd be wrong.

Tommy's idiot friends thought his notes were masterpieces, and my brother was too busy with his own issues to care about mine. Despite Tommy and Theo both having their teams of flunkies, I was completely on my own.

What a wonderful buddy cop film Tommy and Theo would have made: *Bad Cop, Bad Cop*, where the two of them fight crime by annoying bad guys until they give up.

All it takes to be a bully is to find someone vulnerable and be willing to bully them. Tommy and Theo were a little bigger than me, but not by enough to justify their tyranny. Maybe if I still knew some of the older kids, like I did back in Briarwood, Tommy and Theo would have been the ones who were afraid. The reason Tommy and Theo bullied me was because I appeared vulnerable and alone.

At Hunter, no one had my back. If they had, there never would have been a note that said STUPID attached to it.

MY FAVORITE VACUUM

THERE'S AN OLD CLICHÉ THAT THINGS GET WORSE BEFORE they get better. They can also get better before they get worse.

I slowly found my niche at Hunter. I was the quiet kid, and I did everything I could to not be noticed. And then one day, someone noticed how good I was at not being noticed.

Throughout the year, people began pairing off. Being part of a couple made you instantly cool, because someone else had publicly declared you were worth their time. Both members' social stock rose simultaneously. Dating in high school was like two companies investing in each other.

The main benefits of pairing off were that you had someone to sit next to at lunch and slow dance with at the parties where the whole class was invited. Those were the only kind I was invited to, since I was so good at not being noticed. Most of the musical program of those parties consisted of fast dancing. But even the strictest parents would let the DJ play one or two slow songs. And that's when the couples filled the dance floor and put their arms straight out like zombies until their fingertips hardly touched their partner. That didn't matter—the guys were pretty excited that they were grazing the shoulder of an actual, real live girl.

I had accepted that I was not going to be part of the coupling ritual. Cool was not my specialty, and I had yet to see interest from any girls. But one day, someone told me that Alexa Howard "liked" me. I assumed, as any me would in that situation, that I was somehow being tricked. I was pretty sure this was how hunters shot their prey. First they'd spread a rumor about a deer liking another deer to lure the deer into some potentially embarrassing situation and then *BAM*—my head is on a wall in a cabin somewhere. Or stuffed in my locker.

I did want to be liked. I'd started noticing girls when I was still going to school in Briarwood. Well, I'd always noticed girls; but that was more, "Hey, I notice you're in the way of me playing baseball. Could you move?" Suddenly, that changed to, "Hey, I notice that you're in the way of me playing baseball, and that is fine with me because I think you are pretty and thus you can do whatever you want while I awkwardly pretend not to notice you."

My first crush was Linh Phan. I had been in school with her since second grade, and Linh was very much in my way in second grade. I was friends with her brother Quang, and whenever I went to his house, Quang's parents forced us to include Linh.

When we wanted to play baseball or video games or baseball video games, Linh was always in the way. Then one day in sixth grade, *poof*. Linh was not in the way at all.

I was at Anant's house playing a baseball video game when I decided to tell him the big news: that I liked a girl. At the time, it was a very big deal and it made me feel extremely cool. Anant had never liked a girl before, and this was my first time. Being the first in your group to admit you liked someone was the pre-pubescent equivalent of being the first in your group of friends to lose your virginity.

"Oh man, did you hear?" I imagined my leagues of admiring new fans whispering. "Steve has a one-sided attraction to a girl who doesn't care. He's so cool!"

I told Anant all about it, and he asked what I liked about Linh. I am sure I knew words other than nice, smart, and pretty, but I couldn't find them that day. Anant shrugged in support and went back to the game. But I couldn't stop thinking about how much Linh and I had in common—after all, we were both nice and we were both smart. And she was pretty, and I liked looking at pretty girls. We were soul mates.

I finally got the courage to ask Linh out, and I was pretty smooth about it. I told a guy I was kind of friends with to tell a girl Linh was kind of friends with to tell Linh I thought she was pretty. What girl could possibly refuse that display of confidence?

Linh Phan could refuse that display of confidence. And loudly.

When asked if she liked me, Linh said the two letters that would break any boy's heart. Linh did not say *no*. That would have been much more compassionate. Linh said "ew." I wanted to explain to her that it was not a yes-or-no-or-ew question, but I was too busy not speaking to any more girls for a while.

After Linh's rejection heard 'round the world, I was more careful to keep who I liked quiet. I spent my first several months at Hunter with a crush on Rory Daniels. But everyone had a crush on Rory Daniels. She was pretty and smiled all the time, and she had these strange things growing from her chest that magnetized our eyes. To have a crush on Rory was almost cliché. But the first several months of Hunter were a pretty derivative time in my life. After all, I was just trying to fit in.

We sat in assigned seats in math class, and Rory and I were just two desks from each other. And it was in that same class that I learned lots of math skills, like that you can't divide a number by Rory's interest in me.

When you factor in my previous experience with Linh, it's understandable that when word got back to me that Alexa Howard liked me, I didn't believe it. I had never been liked before. But the rumor persisted. Over a week, I heard the rumor from five different people. And the rumor was evolving. It started with Alexa liking me. But in a terrible development, I was told that Alexa wanted to know if I liked her back.

Did I like her back? I was just starting to accept that *she* liked *me.* Now I had to react, and publicly? This was all so sudden. Why must she know right away? DON'T CONTROL ME!

After a week of assuming I was being tricked and a momentary panic when I realized I may not be, I considered the question. Did I like Alexa? I barely knew her. Rory, on the other hand, I knew. I sat kind of near her without speaking to her for months. (Okay, so I didn't know Rory either.) Maybe I did like Alexa. But what I definitely liked was that Alexa liked me. Or that there was a rumor she liked me. Close enough.

I let the rumor mill know I was interested. And I waited for several excruciating hours.

As the lunch period started that day, Alexa approached me in the hallway with a few friends in tow. "I heard you like me," she declared.

Oh no. This is where I get shot and stuffed and mounted above a fireplace.

"Well," she said, "I like you, too."

I wanted to remind her that she had actually liked me first, but I was so relieved this wasn't a trick that I didn't mind the semantics.

"Great," I said. "Want to come with me to lunch?"

And she did. That's how I got my first girlfriend.

I was so excited to tell my friends. If I thought revealing that I was attracted to women was a big deal, imagine the reaction when I told them that one was attracted to me.

Over the last two months of school, I did get to know Alexa, and I really did like her. And not because she liked me, but because she was funny and she had opinions on everything, and there was no one she was afraid to talk to. She was bold and confident and witty. She was already the type of person I wanted to be, and she chose to spend her time with me.

I'm sure Rory didn't mind. She had plenty of other guys who liked her, and she also didn't care that I was a person.

Alexa and I ate lunch together every day, and we zombie danced at obligatory parties, and one day she even kissed me. She lived just a few blocks from Hunter, so she'd walk with me to my yellow bus before she walked home. One day, as we got to the corner, I hugged her goodbye like I always did and before I knew what was happening, her lips were on mine and there was tongue everywhere.

There were a ton of *ooooohs* from other students who saw it happen, like they were in the studio audience of a poorly written sitcom. I didn't care—I was more focused on the extra tongue in my mouth. I was so happy, I'd have skipped all the way to my bus if it hadn't meant getting my ass kicked for skipping.

For the rest of the school year (and the first few weeks of the summer), Alexa and I made out whenever possible. We were terrible at it, but that didn't stop us from trying. We kissed with the passion of soap opera stars and an amount of suction that would have made a vacuum cleaner jealous. I'd never kissed anyone before, so when Alexa tried to suck my tongue clear out of my mouth, I just assumed that was how kissing was supposed to be done.

The physical feeling of kissing Alexa wasn't great—but the emotional feeling was fantastic. Not only was I doing something I didn't think I was cool enough to do, but it also meant that someone liked me enough to kiss me. Or to try to swallow my tongue whole. It was hard to say exactly what Alexa's intent was. And not just because it's impossible to speak without a tongue.

I tried to find us as much privacy as possible. But whether or not we found any, Alexa and I would make out. In Central Park, on the roof of her building, in various corners of our school-yard—we took turns injuring each other's tongues. Until finally, one day, Alexa had to leave.

Before Alexa went to summer camp, she made me promise to write to her every day. "Every day?" I asked, skeptically, wondering if that was just a flourish of speech. "Every day," she said firmly. And so, like many poorly written movie protagonists before me, I stayed true to a romantic gesture that made no actual sense.

I wrote Alexa letters every day for a month, and at first, she did the same. Our letters were generally boring—a summary of our day and gossip if we had any. Some were a full page, some were a few sentences. Regardless of their length or content, the letters were reminders that we were thinking about each other and that we could weather the brutal ten-week storm of summer camp.

Because the postal service is as reliable as, well, the postal service, I'd often not get a letter for a few days and then get them all at once. So it was two weeks before I realized Alexa's letters were getting less frequent. I didn't think it meant anything nefarious—she warned me that her counselors could sometimes be strict about non-camp activities, and I assumed that letter writing could fall under that. I still wrote every day, because that's what someone in a poorly written movie would do.

When you establish a communication pattern with someone you're dating and there's a sudden and drastic change to that pattern, there's always a reason. Occasionally the reason is a change in your significant other's job or in their family or in their hostage situation. More often than not, a change in communication pattern happens because your significant other has become interested in *another* other.

I was heartbroken when I received Alexa's last letter. The letter explained she'd met someone at camp but wanted to date me again after the summer. I realized what I'd feared from the beginning was right: I was being tricked.

The more I thought about it, the more I realized that Alexa didn't like me and she never really had. And, home alone without any more letters to write, I had plenty of time to think about it.

Alexa liked the idea of being in a couple, and she liked the idea of the status it gave her. As all her friends had already coupled up, she figured that if she spread a rumor that she liked the quiet kid, he'd be likely to like her back—every day for most of a summer.

I was always trying to find a private place for us to kiss, but Alexa didn't mind if people saw us. She asked me to write her letters every day so she could get mail in front of people. And now she wanted to receive attention from someone else until she couldn't anymore, at which point she'd go back to receiving it from me. No thank you. Her vacuuming of my tongue had all been a lie. And I wanted no part of it.

I wrote Alexa one last desperate letter just in case I was wrong—telling her that I was hurt and that if she'd rather date this other guy, then that was her choice, but it would mean breaking up. Alexa didn't respond—she didn't need to. She was already getting her attention from someone else.

As I waited for the letter that never came, I thought about it more. I realized that Alexa had never been particularly nice to me. Most of the time she was nice enough. But sometimes her boldness, her confidence, and her wit came at my expense. My own girlfriend made fun of me in public. And that is not okay no matter how much tongue is involved.

While we were dating, I justified her insults. She didn't really mean it—after all, she'd always kiss me in the end. So why risk losing her over my feelings getting hurt occasionally? I had not yet realized that someone who thinks it's funny to hurt your feelings is not worth keeping.

I finally heard from Alexa again a month later, after she returned home. I'm not sure why she called me. If it was to apologize or ask for forgiveness, she didn't get around to doing either.

When Alexa called, she went on and on about how much she enjoyed summer camp, and she even told me that she and her new boyfriend were the most popular couple in camp. She didn't mention her failure to respond to my last letter, how she'd broken my heart, or how she clearly didn't seem hurt at all. Finally, Alexa gave me the chance to speak, when she asked how my summer was.

How was my summer? Alexa knew damn well how my summer was. My summer was terrible. I spent the first half of it missing her and the second half of it mad at myself for missing her. I was angry and hurt and lonely and confused. But I didn't vocalize any of that. I was the quiet kid, after all.

"It wasn't great," I said.

"Well," she casually responded after a bit of silence, brushing off all responsibility for the non-greatness of my summer. "Life sucks."

"Yeah," I fired back. "So do you."

There was no crowd to go wild, no one to give me any high-fives. The only audience to my snarky joke was Alexa, and she certainly didn't appreciate it. But I hadn't said it for her benefit. I'd said it for mine.

Standing up for myself was new to me. And it would be a long time before it became something I was able to do on a regular basis. But in that moment, I was bold and confident and witty. It was just for a moment, but I was the person I wanted to be.

Maybe my summer wasn't so bad after all.

DOWN WITH THE SICKNESS

THE FIRST TIME I WENT TO THE NURSE'S OFFICE, I ACTU-
ally needed to go there. One day in music class, we had a substitute teacher whose idea of teaching was "Don't let the kids kill each other." And he came close to failing.

The poor substitute for a substitute teacher didn't try to teach or even to distract us. He just let us occupy ourselves however we wanted. Some of the kids pulled their desks together to gossip. Others doodled. Some read. I went to the back of the room to join a few other students who were playing cards.

Playing cards was one of the ways I was social at Hunter. I was good at it, and you don't need to be popular or charming to be a solid card player. You don't even need to speak. If you doubt that statement, watch any hour of the World Series of Poker and you'll see that misfits are welcome.

Our game of choice was Ding Pai, a bastardized version of Pai Gow poker where you win by playing all your cards before the other players. I won that day, if you can call getting slapped in the face winning.

My classsmate did not slap me purposely. He was about to play his last cards, and I played mine on the turn right before his. He threw his hands up in anger and disbelief, and the back of one of them crashed into my nose with the ferocity of a drunken monkey taking a driver's test. Or of someone who had just lost at Ding Pai to the quiet kid.

I'd had nosebleeds before and was very familiar with the ball-up-tissue-and-plug-your-nose methodology. But if I'd tried that, the school would have been out of tissues. I'd never seen so much blood.

This nosebleed was different from what I was used to. This was a lot of blood, a lot of pain, and a lot of fear. I wasn't scared—I was too distracted by the pain and the blood to be scared. But the substitute teacher was terrified.

"Get him to the nurse's office!" the sub bellowed, knowing that children with broken noses have a tendency to ruin performance reviews. If this got out, he may never be allowed to pretend to teach again—he'd be left drawing hand turkeys all by himself.

I didn't even know there was a nurse's office, but one of the other students led me there as I left a Hansel and Gretel–esque blood trail behind me in the hallway.

As awful as the hallway looked (one teacher described it as a "war zone"), my nose wasn't as bad as I thought. Nurse Marion calmly stopped the bleeding and determined that my nose was not broken. And then, instead of sending me to my next class, Nurse Marion asked if I wanted to lie down. After all, I'd had a tough day, and I could use some time to recover.

Lie down? Instead of going to class? Absolutely. I dare you to find one high school student who would answer that question differently. I was led into a room with three cots, chose one, shut the lights off, and took a nap. My god, it was glorious. *Sleeping in school—I should have thought of this years ago.*

Nurse Marion was a kind woman in her forties. At least, I think she was in her forties. When you're fourteen, everyone older than twenty-five seems like they're in their forties. But no matter how old she was, Nurse Marion was kind. She was calm and spoke in a quiet, measured manner, and she made me feel like nothing else could hurt me. The nurse's office was a place to heal—physically and emotionally.

The "incident of my not-quite-broken nose" was the first time I went to the nurse's office, but it would not be the last. I didn't get slapped in the face again, at least not physically. But I did fall.

Theo still hadn't physically hurt me, but one day Tommy did. During a class period while we waited for our teacher to arrive, Tommy and Theo were being particularly vicious. Tommy was calling my red hair *gay* over and over, because he was that sort of intelligent, forward-thinking gentleman. And Theo was balling up his fist and glaring at me, as if he was going to start wailing on me in the middle of social studies.

Tommy affixed a GAY note to my back, which I removed, and

I walked to the trash with the intention of throwing it away. That walk would give me twenty seconds away from the bad cop twins and get me that much closer to the teacher arriving and Tommy and Theo having to shut up for a blissful forty minutes.

I was sitting back down when Tommy yanked my chair out from under me. As I fell, everyone laughed. When they heard my head crack against the seat, they stopped laughing. Except for Tommy and Theo, who probably high-fived. They had the teamwork to make their dreams work.

I lay there, dazed. My fall sounded worse than it felt, and I mainly stayed down because if I got up, Tommy and Theo would start in on me again. When the teacher came in, he demanded to know what had happened.

"Steve fell and hit his head," I heard an anonymous girl say. She wasn't wrong, but that was like summarizing a fairy tale by saying, "Hansel and Gretel went for a walk, then made lunch." Not really the most important details of the story.

That weak summation of events led my teacher to send me to the nurse's office, which was way better than a twenty-second walk to the trash can. I was rid of Tommy and Theo for an entire class period as Nurse Marion made sure the bump on my head was just a bump on my head.

Thus began a tradition for me. When the bullying got too difficult, I'd fake illness and head over to Nurse Marion. She'd always have hot tea for my throat or a quiet cot for a nap or whatever I needed for whatever I was faking that day. I doubt that Nurse Marion believed I was really sick that often; more likely she saw through my shenanigans and was giving me a break.

Disappearing into the nurse's office was an extension of what I'd done since I was a kid; I faked being sick a few times a year in grade school, too. When the day was too nice to spend indoors, or I felt like sleeping longer, or I wanted to play atop a snow-covered car, I worked on my acting chops and convinced my mother that school just wasn't the best idea for me that day. Sometimes I even convinced myself I was sick, only to miraculously recover by around two P.M. I must have had the eight-hour flu.

At Hunter, the nurse's office became my sanctuary. The school kept track of absences, but they did not keep track of how many periods one student skipped to get some respite from bullies. All I had to do to avoid getting caught was alternate which periods I skipped. As long as I kept rotating classes, I could go to the nurse's office one class period a week, and no teacher would ever get suspicious. This was way better than taking full days off from school. These were like mini vacations that no one knew about— they were things to look forward to.

For most people, the idea of a school-issued cot in a room with fluorescent lights left on does not sound like a vacation. But when your alternative is Tommy and Theo, Nurse Marion's sounds like a beach cabana in the Bahamas.

When I was in the nurse's office, there were no puerile signs on my back or hypothetical fists coming at me. There was tea and sleep and, most importantly, quiet.

Spending that much time in the nurse's office was as good of an idea as unscrewing the check engine light bulb in your car. It helped in the short term but was extremely dangerous in the long run.

I was missing class, which made my grades slip. The number of Ds I got with messages that said something like *try harder* increased. I went from occasionally being unprepared to being at risk of failing some of my classes.

Meanwhile, and much worse, I was actually getting sick.

It wasn't until many years later that I learned I'd developed an eating disorder. I have what is known as eating disorder not otherwise specified (EDNOS), because the majority of the medical community has yet to get past anorexia and bulimia. And before you say, *But Steve, you look great!,* my EDNOS has nothing to do with how I look; my EDNOS is about how I feel. Also, thank you for saying I look great.

I wanted to buy some time away from my bullies. Years of constantly pretending I was sick manifested itself in the ability to throw up on cue. I willed myself to actually be sick. Something in my head snapped, and I started associating throwing up with feeling better. Whenever I was stressed, nervous, or anything else that can cause the average person a bit of nausea, I'd begin to believe I was sick and consequently throw up. It's quite a skill, though one that is impossible to monetize. What a horrible carnival act.

For almost a decade, I did not know what was wrong with me. I saw specialists, went to hospitals, and took tests with cameras shoved down my throat all because I couldn't conceive that this was a mental problem. I wanted there to be a physical reason this was happening beyond my control. I didn't want to admit that this was a setback of my own creation.

Finally a friend who'd studied in the field of eating disorders woke me up to what was happening. At first I rejected the premise—how could I have an eating disorder? I'd seen *very special* episodes of various sitcoms and none of them applied to me. I'm a *man*. According to sitcom and after-school-special writers, men don't have eating disorders. But the more I thought about it, did the research, and spoke to professionals, the more my friend's diagnosis made sense. And the more I realized I was being ridiculous. Of course men can have eating disorders. I was one of them.

I have been fighting against this disorder ever since. Eating disorders are like your first love: Despite how sick they make you, you're never truly over them. An eating disorder is a lifetime battle; you just learn to defeat it more often than it defeats you.

I have my methods of handling things—eating healthy and at reasonable hours, getting a decent amount of sleep, and attacking stress with a que será, será attitude. But I still fight the battle a few times a year. My EDNOS typically comes on late at night, when I'm in the least control of my thoughts. If I can just get to sleep, I am always better in the morning. But getting to sleep without giving in—sometimes that can be more difficult than I can ever explain to someone who hasn't fought a similar battle. Explaining how EDNOS works to someone who has never experienced it is more difficult than explaining every *Game of Thrones* character to someone who has never seen the show.

My EDNOS began because I was learning to run from my problems instead of learning how to face them. Leaving for an hour wasn't helping me get bullied any less. The strides I'd made in self-confidence when I stood up to Alexa had disappeared. People like Theo and Tommy were making my life harder. But I was making it worse.

This was more than flinching. I'd unknowingly become my own bully.

THE WIND
IS GONE

MY BULLIES HAD ANOTHER THING IN COMMON—THEY were part of a group at Hunter nicknamed The Clique. Here's a rule: Any time a group nicknames themselves, it's a pretty good idea to stay away from that group.

We've all known one kid who returned from summer break and told everyone to call them something like A-Dawg. Sure, Alfred. We'll call you SOMETHING that starts with A.

Hell, we had trouble when Ricky abruptly told us to call him Rick. So how is it that a group gets to nickname themselves? It works because there's power in numbers, especially when the rest of us are scared of those numbers.

The Clique was made up of students who had come up through the elementary school together. These kids had eight years to bond before they met any of the rest of us. So when we arrived at school and a close-knit group of twenty confident (and mostly attractive) strangers told us that they were called The Clique, no one questioned them.

As the years passed, The Clique would absorb more members,

like the poisonous gas cloud that it was. One of these new members was Scarlet Daly.

Scarlet Daly quickly became the Regina George of The Clique. She was a classic Mean Girl—extremely beautiful on the outside and extremely cruel on the inside.

Long after I had graduated from Hunter, I toured a lion's enclosure, where I was about ten feet from a lion with nothing between us but my clothes and fear pee. That lion reminded me of Scarlet Daly. Majestic, beautiful, lacking interest in me, and capable of tearing me to shreds.

If you need any more explanation as to the type of person Scarlet was, she ended up marrying Tommy Tillet.

Stephanie Spencer was another member of The Clique, but she wasn't like the rest of them. She seemed kind and genuine and even smiled at me (or she was already smiling while I happened to look in her direction). I never spoke to her—but her smile was enough for me to decide I liked her.

I did everything I could to hide my crush: staring at Stephanie constantly, making sure to sit as close to her as possible, and instantly and obviously changing the subject whenever Stephanie's name was mentioned. The only way anyone could possibly tell that I had a crush on Stephanie was if they had eyes or ears or a basic understanding of human behavior.

When the rumors started, I denied them with the amount of defensiveness that equates to admitting something. I denied it so hard that if I'd said, "Yes, I am madly in love with Stephanie Spencer," fewer people would have thought I had feelings for her.

I didn't want it to get back to Stephanie that I liked her—a guy like me wasn't going to get a girl like her. Her knowing I liked her would accomplish nothing other than her sitting farther away from me in class and growing stingier with her smiles. I had nothing to gain and the bright spot in my morning to lose.

The most important thing was to prevent the news of my crush from getting back to Scarlet. Letting Scarlet know that I liked one of the members of her pride would be like walking toward the lion waving my arms, covered in zebra blood, and also being a zebra.

Then one day, it happened. The Steve-likes-Stephanie rumor was getting top billing in my high school hallway. I knew it was temporary; rumor mills never stay on the same subject for more than two or three days. All I really needed to do was stall until a new rumor came out that would bury mine. Maybe a teacher would make out with a student or the school would close due to an E. coli outbreak or World War III would start. Or, more likely, someone else's crush would become newer, juicier gossip. I just had to avoid the lion until then. But life doesn't always work out the way you want it to.

Appropriately, it was during lunch when Scarlet confronted me in the hall. She was hungry for zebra, and it was feeding time.

"Steve, you need to stop pestering Stephanie," Scarlet said to me as if quietly walking away when Stephanie smiled at me was somehow pestering her.

At least she didn't call me Steven.

"You need to take your gross red self and stick to playing chess with your nerdy friends."

That's where Scarlet was wrong. I didn't play chess *or* have friends.

I didn't get the chance to speak during Scarlet's tirade. She went on ad nauseam about how ridiculous I was for thinking I had a chance with Stephanie. After all, a guy like me wasn't going to get a girl like her. Scarlet was right about that part, but there was no need to say it. Ad nauseam is the correct expression, because the whole thing made me want to go to the nurse's office.

I knew I didn't have a chance with Stephanie—I already told you that a page ago. But I still enjoyed Stephanie's smile and wanted to sit near her. And as long as I kept it to myself, my crush was none of Scarlet's business. I wasn't following Stephanie between classes or passing her unwanted love notes. I wasn't even really sitting near Stephanie—I always sat a few desks away. I was simply an unpopular boy who had the audacity to exist near a popular girl.

Finally, Scarlet finished telling me how worthless I was, and it was my turn to respond. By this time, dozens of my classmates had gathered around to watch. I'm sure some felt bad for me. I'm sure some were there to cheer her on. Most were likely somewhere in between. But I am definitely sure that most were watching in the way that, when we stumble on a nature documentary, it's hard to stop watching until after the zebra is dead.

Then I saw one face in the crowd that stood out. It was Stephanie—standing rank and file behind Scarlet.

Had Stephanie put Scarlet up to this? Did Stephanie know this would happen? Was she enjoying watching me get verbally eviscerated? This was the first time I wasn't happy to see Stephanie's smile. And then it hit me. I knew exactly what my response would be. And it would be glorious.

I believe that everyone's mind is like a computer, and each of us has a varied combination of storage and processing speed. My propensity for analogies like this are one of the reasons a guy like me couldn't get a girl like Stephanie.

The reason I have always been fast on my feet is because my mind-computer can access files very quickly. Often my files aren't as in-depth as someone else's, and I certainly don't have more of them. But I can get to each one very rapidly. The problem was that, when I was fourteen, I had very few files that covered social interaction. Sure, I had files on the New York Mets and babysitting and the old movies my parents let me watch. I had the ability to be quick but nothing relevant to say. Imagine what Sherlock Holmes's power of deductive reasoning would look like if he didn't have any relevant knowledge to draw from.

I noticed the scratch on the left side of your glasses and the scuff on the same side of your boots. It's clear that you have scuffed your boot and scratched your glasses.

Brilliant deduction, Holmes.

I was standing there in that hallway faced with my personal Regina George, in front of a growing percentage of my high school student body, and I was given a moment to come back at her. With one perfect response, I could shift the balance of power forever. If I could outsmart and outwit Scarlet, a guy like me *could* get a girl like Stephanie. Probably not Stephanie herself, since she might have been in on this, but someone else. This wasn't a physical fight—this was a battle of wits, the thing in the world that I am best at. I just needed the perfect comeback, and I needed it quickly. I was so sure I had it.

Scarlet had just spent the better part of five minutes reminding me of the pecking order and putting me in my place in front of an eager crowd. She expected me to lay down and take the beating. To have no answer other than a sheepish, "Yes, ma'am." To cower before this queen of the hallway jungle. But Scarlet didn't count on my ability to think on my feet. It was my turn to flip the food chain on its head.

"Frankly, Scarlet," I said, followed by an exaggerated pause to make my knock-out blow land even harder, "I don't give a damn."

I expected a chorus of *oooooohs*, a round of high fives, and for various people to inform Scarlet that she had, in fact, been served. It didn't quite go that way. The *oooooohs* were replaced by stunned silence. The round of high fives were replaced by confused looks. And no one outside the cafeteria was being served. As it turns out, most teenagers aren't impressed by a good *Gone with the Wind* reference.

Scarlet broke the silence by laughing—not with what I said, but at it. The crowd disbursed, having seen the devouring they came to see. Scarlet had been the mean girl they all assumed she was, and I'd been the nerd they assumed I was. The food chain had not been altered. The red-headed zebra carcass lay before them, unable to change his stripes.

I stopped trying to sit near Stephanie after that. And I don't know whether or not she kept smiling, because I refused to make eye contact. I just went about my day, quietly grazing far from the lions, thankful that I wasn't swallowed whole. I may have been embarrassed in the hallway, but it could have been much worse. They could have given me a nickname.

I don't think I could have faced high school being called Vivien Leigh.

HUMBUCKERS AND WAWA PEDALS

I HAVE ALWAYS BEEN VERY MUSICALLY INCLINED. I could read sheet music from a young age, and at four, my mother caught me playing a concerto on her piano.

All of that is a lie. I am a musical idiot, and sheet music looks like Braille to me. When I was four, my mother caught me damaging her piano by hitting it repeatedly with my brother's flute. I don't even know if concertos are played on pianos. Or with flutes.

But ten years later, I started hanging out with Jacob Corry. Jacob and I were in the same class, and he was one of the few people in that class who wasn't a complete jerk to me. The thing I liked most about Jacob was his obsession with music. Also, I liked that he wasn't a complete jerk to me.

Before Jacob, my relationship with music was simple. Someone played it and I listened. But music was certainly cool. And if you could play guitar, man, you were the coolest. Or so I imagined.

See that kid wearing the wrong-sized, flannel, hand-me-down shirt? He can play the first few chords of three different songs. He's the coolest.

Jacob took guitar lessons a few times a week, and he was *good*. Like, really good. Like, people should not be that good at anything good. And Jacob tried to teach me.

This became our ritual—I'd go over to Jacob's apartment after school, and he'd teach me whatever I was able to learn, which wasn't much. I parroted Jacob's opinions that Gibsons were better than Fenders and electric was more fun than acoustic and Joe Satriani was a god. I had never heard of Joe Satriani outside of the context of Jacob discussing him, but after I looked him up, sure, he was the best.

Sometimes we'd go to the Sam Ash on Queens Boulevard, where anyone could play the instruments they had for sale. Jacob would pick up a thousand-dollar guitar and play something great on it. And then I would very carefully pick up a hundred-dollar guitar and play the four chords he taught me: C, G, D, and e minor. If I wanted to get fancy, I'd change the order. And when Sam Ash was selling a Steve Vai autographed guitar, I pretended to be very impressed. I had never heard of Steve Vai outside of the context of Jacob discussing him.

Eventually I learned bar chords and power chords and even hammering on and pulling off. I was never proficient, but I became competent. The time had come for me to get my own guitar. Since I couldn't afford more than packets of ramen for lunch, that was going to prove difficult.

Music was not foreign in my house. My mother played many instruments, including guitar. I really did damage her piano, which was particularly awful of me because she made extra money giving piano lessons. After the piano incident, I stayed away from my mother's musical instruments. It was pretty easy to stay away because my mother had no interest in any music written after 1965.

My mother didn't even like the good, pre-1965 stuff. There were no Beatles in my house. There were Penguins and Alley Cats and Blue Jays and Spaniels and Flamingos. But no Beatles. My mother loved two genres of music: folk and doo-wop. And neither one of those were cool.

No one in history has said, "See that kid wearing the wrong-sized, flannel, hand-me-down shirt? He can play the first few chords of Earth Angel. He's cool." More likely they've said, "See that kid wearing the wrong-sized, flannel, hand-me-down shirt? He can play the first few chords of Earth Angel. Let's get him."

I had nothing against folk music—I could appreciate Peter, Paul, and/or Mary, and folk spawned Bob Dylan, Joni Mitchell, Paul Simon, James Taylor, and other people whose last names are also first names. But I didn't want to play folk music. I wanted to rock. Maybe it's called folk music because your folks like it.

My mother had an extra guitar, partially because she had an

extra one of everything she rarely used. I asked if I could have it. The neck was chipped, it needed new strings, and the only way I could make it rock was to break it onstage (as if it wasn't already broken enough). But my mother said yes, and suddenly I had a real guitar. And suddenly, the one-hundred dollar guitars at Sam Ash looked super-expensive by comparison.

I took my new, deformed baby to Sam Ash and had it restrung. I don't know whether they were more surprised that someone was spending money on such a piece of garbage or that Jacob and I were spending money at all. But I had a guitar and that was all that mattered. And Jacob was kind enough to stop telling me that electric was more fun than acoustic. Considering the guitar I had, there was no need to rub it in.

Even once I had my own guitar to practice on, I wasn't very good. I could never get my fingers fully calloused like Jacob could, and sheet music still read like Braille to me (which is probably harder to read with calloused fingers). But simply having a guitar to poorly noodle on gave me the street cred to start hanging out in what was affectionately known as the Freak Hallway.

Hunter High School's hallways are shaped like a Q. The vast majority of high school and *Lord of the Flies* takes place in that O-shaped part of the Q. But in that little nubbin that extended out and transformed the O into the Q, that's where the freaks hung out.

The freaks weren't freaks so much as they were artists. They were painters and theater kids and guitar players. They were

people who didn't fit in with the cliques of the world and preferred to exit the popularity rat race rather than run behind it.

Hunter's name for the Q nubbin was the Art Hallway, as the
art classroom was right there. But at some point in Hunter's
history, one of the popular kids called everyone in that hallway a bunch of freaks, and the freaks proudly adopted the
moniker.

I desperately wanted to fit in with the kids that didn't fit
in, and that's where my new guitar helped. I'd sit in the Freak
Hallway during lunch, alternating between packets of ramen
and plucking my guitar. I quietly played the few things I
knew how to play, attempting to mask my lack of knowledge, talent, and confidence. The Freak Hallway was a much
healthier escape than the nurse's office, and it allowed me to
overhear conversations that made me realize that other people's lives sucked, too. Every now and then, I'd even make a
friend.

Most of the freaks had walls up, solidly constructed from
years of bullying. So most of the friendships I made were brief
and superficial. But we were all, at the very least, kind to one
another.

One day as I was silently pretending to play my guitar, a
senior sat down next to me.

"Mind if I play a little?" the stranger said.

"Sure," I responded, handing him the worst guitar he had ever
held.

"Let me show you something," he started strumming. "You know how to do basic chords, like C-D-G-e minor?"

"Of course," I said, concealing the fact that they were pretty much all I knew. "Who doesn't know C-D-G and e minor?"

"Well," he went on, "C-D-G-e minor is the basis for most hit songs."

I was familiar with this—it was the reason Jacob taught those chords to me. But the senior played way more than I knew: Green Day, Bush, Blues Traveler, Johnny Cash, Pearl Jam, Lynyrd Skynyrd, John Denver, Bob Dylan, and . . . the Penguins.

He showed me that Earth Angel's G-em-C-D was virtually the same as Green Day's G-D-em-C.

And that was the nature of the Freak Hallway. Fourteen-year-old computer nerds and seventeen-year-old goth kids sat and ate lunch together. Because, like doo-wop and punk, the basic elements of the song were still the same.

THE MARTIN LUTHER KING JR. DAY SALE

THE HOUSE I GREW UP IN WAS EXTREMELY LARGE relative to my family's economic success, which was small. Real estate agents would have described it as having great bones. It did, in the way that after someone dies you can see their bones.

The other houses on the block were all much nicer, but they were also much smaller. The house to the left of ours was even being completely redone. That way their house would have a ton of curb appeal, as long as you didn't look just to the right at ours.

My parents needed a big house because they had four kids, but also because my parents loved stuff. The great thing about a big ugly house is that it can fit so much stuff, your kids will be ashamed of inviting anyone over. My parents' love for stuff is why I always went to Jacob's apartment. It was easier to play guitar when there was room to move.

What kinds of stuff did my parents have? All the stuff. Our basement and parts of our first floor were covered in scary piles of what most people would refer to as garbage but what the Hofstetters called possessions. We had the slate of a pool table permanently propped up against the wall under a sheet. We had a bolt of denim in our dining room. And we had the old, used carpet from my synagogue, in case we ever decided to carpet a twenty-thousand-square-foot building in the style of the 1970s. This was not a place I wanted to show anyone.

Most adults don't know what a bolt of denim is. A child with no interest in the sewing arts certainly shouldn't know what a bolt of denim is. But I knew what a bolt of denim was because my parents were pack rats. They were not hoarders, but they could see the exit ramp to Hoardtown. Most of the stuff they kept was not completely worthless, as it could easily fetch a nickel at a yard sale. If an item had some value to someone somewhere, my parents held on to it. As they say—one man's trash is another man's bolt of denim.

The best way to explain my parents' desire to keep everything is that, at one point, my mother had two copies of a book called *Organize Yourself!* Two separate people in her life saw that book and knew that they needed to buy it for her. And my mother, in the most Hofstetter way possible, kept those two copies of *Organize Yourself!* on different shelves.

Even the real stuff we had was often broken. Our TV was a decade past being old, and when the screen inevitably started flipping, we had to know exactly which part of the TV to smack to get it working. Our microwave was fixed in a similar fashion. Unfortunately, our VCR and stereo didn't have good spots to hit, so those just sat there broken. But every now and then we actually got new stuff. Nothing nice—just new.

That January, my mother took us shopping over the holiday weekend. Not New Year's weekend—Martin Luther King Jr. Day weekend. Even then, I found the idea of a Martin Luther King Jr. Day sale tacky. Beth was adopted and black, so we learned about Martin Luther King Jr. early. Dr. King dreamed of a future where his four children could be judged not by the color of their skin but by the content of their character. There was no part in that dream that described one-day sales. Especially not white sales.

I didn't get to go shopping much, so that trip was not the time for civil disobedience. We were a hand-me-down family, and the only time we ever bought anything new was when we absolutely had to. That's what this trip was—I was taller than my siblings, cousins, and many people my age, and I was growing quickly. I was low on winter clothes, so my mother used the sales as a way to save a bit of money on keeping me warm. It's what Dr. King would have wanted.

"I have a dream," Dr. King once said, probably not followed by "where one of my four children will outgrow the other three and have to get his own winter coat."

When we returned from our winter clothing expedition, we knew our house had been broken into immediately. There was no way to tell if it had been recently ransacked, as it always looked ransacked. Our big break-in clue was that the back door was cut in half. Someone had taken an axe (or something that functioned similarly to an axe) and chopped half of the door clear off. And my older brother, David, had somehow slept through it.

I have to applaud the burglars on the creativity of their break-in. First, they broke in on Martin Luther King Jr. Day. Most burglars would choose more obvious shopping holidays like Black Friday or literally any other day of the year. But these guys knew that the Hofstetters couldn't resist the bargains being offered in the name of the most important civil rights leader in history.

Also, most burglars break a window or check for an unlocked door like a bunch of uncreative hacks. Only the truly inventive burglars contemplate a wood door's weakness. And wood's obvious weakness is an axe. Though perhaps they used a chainsaw—David is a heavy sleeper.

We pieced together that someone had broken in very loudly, but David didn't think anything of it because of the ongoing construction next door. He heard a loud noise and just rolled over and went back to sleep. Shortly after that, a phone call did wake David up. Him walking to my parents' room to pick up the call must have spooked the burglars, who fled. While walking to the phone, David heard some people downstairs, and he heard them leave when he picked up the phone. He just assumed the burglars were us, on our way to score some savings in the name of racial equality.

Despite their axe-capades, the burglars didn't have much time in the house alone, so they grabbed what they could. And what they could grab was my Nintendo and all my games. Damn it! That was the one thing I owned that could get friends to come over and ignore the bolt of denim.

The axmen also managed to steal the broken stereo and the broken VCR. Seriously, that's all they took. They were probably cursing themselves as they left that they didn't have time to grab the bolt of denim.

I would love to have seen the look on the thieves' faces when they walked into our big house and saw nothing of value. And not just nothing of value, but everything of not value.

"I'm sure there's jewelry in here somewhere," one would say, after breathlessly emptying my mother's drawers. "It's probably behind these eight giant rolls of used seventies-style carpet."

Retail, I was burgled out of $800 worth of stuff. But the two things I lost that were worth the most were my time and my feeling of security. It was all the Saturday nights I'd spent earning that money that mattered.

I'd wasted so much time working to make the money for what they stole. If I could have had those nights back, imagine all the parties I could have not gone to. Okay, babysitting was actually a pretty great way to spend my time.

To have all the results of your hard work completely stripped away is a terrible feeling. In Greek mythology, Sisyphus is punished by being forced to roll a boulder uphill, watch it roll back down, and then roll it back up again. The reason that's such a harsh punishment is because hard work is particularly awful when it produces no results. And this thief had just eliminated all of my results. The burglar made sure that I'd been babysitting uphill.

The feeling of security they stole from me was even more important. According to the first crime statistic I lazily googled, one in every thirty-six homes in America gets broken into each year, so you will probably experience a home invasion sometime in your life. And it's pretty awful. The idea that someone could be in your home without your permission is terrifying no matter how little your property is worth.

It took me a few weeks before I could get a good night's sleep again. I jumped at every sound as if it were another axe. I'd wake up frantically and ask David if he heard anything. He wouldn't reply, because he'd be fast asleep.

The break-in wasn't all bad. Aside from learning that David owning an alarm clock is utterly pointless, I learned my parents had theft insurance. Theft insurance made sense in a neighborhood where people break doors in half with axes. I wished the thieves had stolen the denim and the carpet just to confuse the insurance adjusters. Also, so it would have been gone and I could actually have friends over.

It took several months, but eventually the insurance company paid the full value it would have cost to replace my games, and I spent it on something more important to me.

My parents gave me the full $800, which was more money

than I'd ever seen at once before. And possibly more money than I'd ever seen in total before. Fearing I might blow it on something silly like an amazing unforgettable experience instead of pointless physical stuff, my parents made a rule against that. I was told that since the money was to replace the possessions that had been taken from me, I was to spend it on replacing those possessions.

If there's one thing my parents believed in, it was the perceived value of possessions. I was tempted to ask my parents how much they wanted for the bolt of denim, but I did not want to lose the money completely.

After buying some decent strings for my guitar, for the first time in my life, I spent money on my appearance. I bought new clothes. And not from Goodwill or the Salvation Army or a neighbor's yard sale, but actual new clothes. They were still on the discount rack, but they were new and they were mine. I also bought deodorant and cologne. If I was going to look fresh, I should smell that way, too.

My mother accused me of going back on my promise to only buy tangible items, since deodorant and cologne were perishable. She also questioned what a fourteen-year-old kid needed with cologne. I did my best to explain to her that a fourteen-year-old is not a kid but a person.

I was enough of a person to babysit actual children, to play a musical instrument, and to have had (and lost) a girlfriend. I was a person that was judged and shamed and bullied by other people. I spent my money to buy Right Guard rather than Street Fighter because all the Hadoukens in the world wouldn't stop a bully from teasing me. But not smelling like I'd just been in a street fight might.

Considering what happened to our door, I should have also bought some Axe.

The break-in ended up being a positive experience for me. The thieves stole my sense of comfort, but I replaced it with a sense of style. The thieves stole my sense of pride in my work, but I replaced it with a sense of pride in my appearance.

Most importantly, I learned two things my parents should have already known: "stuff" isn't that important and nothing good can come of going to a sale on Martin Luther King Jr. Day.

THE LONG RIDE
ON THE SHORT BUS

BECAUSE HUNTER HAD STUDENTS FROM ALL OVER NEW
York City, buses were often segregated by borough, and usually
by neighborhood. We didn't have *the* school bus—we had several
small, competing bus companies, and they were all those mini,
five-row buses. There's a delicious irony that at one of the top
academic schools in the country, everyone took the short bus.

My first bus to Hunter was relatively quiet, because it was
run by a very professional bussing company. The bus driver
couldn't have been cast better—she was an old, angry, no-non-
sense woman who made Rosie the Riveter look like June Cleaver.
She chain-smoked and barked orders at us, and if we weren't
outside waiting when she got to our houses in the morning, she just left. My first bus was quiet and always on time
because we were scared to test the driver. Because she was a
professional.

But, like my mother did with many things in our lives, she

looked at my bussing situation and thought, "Is there a way we could save money on this by making it worse?"

That was the Hofstetter mantra. If there was a way we could spend less but still accomplish the bare minimum of the same result, we found a way. We went to school clad in ugly hand-me-downs. We ate store-brand everything. My father added an hour every day on his already two-hour commute driving the company carpool. And so, my mother set out to save a very little bit of money by risking my life.

First, my mother found a bus service that charged less than the one we'd been using. I'm not sure how she found them —perhaps on a matchbook or a bathroom wall. Maybe out of desperation, my mother dialed 1-800-BUS-THIS, and this company happened to pick up. This was before Yelp. Had Yelp already been in existence by then, I'd assume that my mother had found these people by searching for the bus company with the fewest stars.

The new company my mother found was the opposite of professional, and they had only one bus. If they were a bus company, what was their plan before my mother called? It's possible that my mother dialed a wrong number and whoever picked up said, "yeah, sure we've got a bus," and, after they'd hung up, scrambled to find one like the RV in *Breaking Bad*.

Once my mother had locked in a bus "company," she had to meet their minimum number of fourteen students. Hunter had a student directory with everyone's address and phone number. So, one by one, my mother called every single Hunter student in Queens to pitch their parents on her bussing plan. Every single Queens Hunter student, regardless of grade, got a call from my mother.

I'm sure she used other words, but what her call meant was obvious: "Hi, this is Steven Hofstetter's mother. When your parents get home, can you have them give me a call back? I just wanted to see if your family was as cheap as mine is, and to make sure that Steven would be bullied this upcoming year. Also, now you know that we don't call him Steve, so you don't have to either."

My mother found nine other equally cheap families, which wasn't quite enough. Rather than give up and allow me to continue to travel to school in the least bullied way possible, my mother had an epiphany that would also negatively affect my sister Beth. Perfect.

Geniuses always know where they were when they first had the idea that changed everything. I am sure that Alexander Graham Bell knew where he was when he invented the telephone and the same could be said for Albert Einstein when he first thought of the theory of relativity. When my mother came up with the brilliant idea that could socially stunt two of her children at once, she was sitting on the living room couch with a legal pad.

My sister Beth was also going to be going to school in Manhattan that year. Beth and I could have each taken the subway with some of our classmates, but that was way too dangerous for my mother's sensibilities. Instead, my mother came up with the idea of combining buses.

Including Beth, there were four kids from our area going to her school, just enough to make the minimum of fourteen. And so, like many other poorly thought-out plans before it, our own little short bus became a reality.

The first week of school that year was brutal. "Your mom" jokes sting so much more when the perpetrator has just gotten off the phone with her.

What made my mother's bussing-for-bullies plan even more ridiculous is that Hunter has a program where all students get free subway passes. Had my mother not been over-protective, I could have been coolly taking the subway with some of the other students for free. But in her mind, the subway was way too dangerous. So instead, we hired a fly-by-night bus service. For safety.

At first, our driver was the owner of the bus company, a woman in her thirties named Mirta. Mirta was large and loud and LOVED gossiping with the kids. Sometimes she'd be at my house at seven A.M. and sometimes she'd be there at seven-thirty, so we all learned to stay inside until she sent one of the other kids out to knock on our door. Seatbelts were as optional as scheduled pick-up times.

The only benefit of that bus was becoming friendly with another student named Ozzie. Ozzie was much cooler than I was, and the only reason he was bussed in is because he lived too far from the nearest subway station. Under most circumstances,

Ozzie and I would not have become friends. But Ozzie was the only other Mirta student in my grade, and we bonded over our mutual fear for our safety. It was like going through war together, complete with an insane general.

Mirta spent most of the drives playing the radio loudly, and whenever anyone took a lane without signaling, she'd roll down the window and yell "Hit my bus, I need the money!" It was very entertaining to see how stupefied the average person was when they saw a school bus driver challenging them to an accident.

And then, things got ridiculous.

Mirta began replacing herself a few days a week with one of her employees, Valerio. Valerio was Mirta's nephew, a man in his early twenties who clearly couldn't have held any other job—or this one if he hadn't been related to Mirta. Valerio often bragged to us about how after he dropped us off he'd have sex on the bus. One morning, we were all picked up super-early and he flew through traffic at insane speeds. We got to school almost an hour before class because there was a nurse Valerio wanted to meet after his shift. Because he was a professional.

One afternoon while we were stuck in traffic, a kid hit our bus with a snowball. Valerio opened the bus door and started yelling at him. Valerio then told us to chase after the kid—and we did. A group of four teenagers stormed off the bus and chased a strange kid into the Grant Houses—projects in Harlem. When we got to the building, we realized where we were, and we raced back to the bus to find Valerio doubled over with laughter.

What a hilarious prank! He had convinced four teenagers whose safety he was responsible for to chase a child into an unfamiliar neighborhood! Oh man, if he could have seen the look on our faces when we realized our lives were in danger! Classic!

My mother was too concerned for my well-being to let me take the subway to school. The way Valerio drove that bus, it would have been much safer for me to take the subway. By myself. Naked. In February.

Despite Valerio and Mirta's hijinks, they didn't physically injure any of us. But the driver of the car that hit our bus did.

That day's ride was otherwise uneventful. Mirta was paying more attention to the radio than she was to any of us, and we stopped at a traffic light. The person coming up behind us didn't stop until metal on metal forced him to. Mirta finally got her wish. Someone had hit her bus.

Because we were a school bus (and because Mirta needed the money), the cops and paramedics were called. My back was a bit sore, so I spoke up. I was a mix of genuinely hurt and wanting to be hurt, but was relieved to escape my school bus. One of the paramedics spent the rest of that afternoon trying to make me laugh. Once we were on the ambulance, he kept pointing out crazy things that were allegedly going on just outside the window that I could have seen if only I hadn't been strapped down. That ambulance was great—it was like the nurse's office with wheels, but funnier. I was too distracted to concentrate on the pain—laughter was powerful stuff.

I wasn't scared in the hospital because the paramedic continued to excitedly point out things I couldn't see. According to him, there was a nurse with enormous breasts and a low-cut uniform right behind me—too bad I couldn't turn my head. "Here she comes! Don't look now!" he said. I wondered if this was a recurring gag he did or if that paramedic just thought of the bit for me. Either way, I had a pretty wonderful time getting hit by a car. Valerio would have loved that nurse.

The doctor who examined me recommended I take two days off from school. I didn't protest—four-day weekends were not something I ever argued with.

The other driver's insurance sent Mirta a check to cover the damage to her bus. Of course, she pocketed that money, which made it easier to find the bus after school—we just looked for the one with the giant dent in the rear fender.

The insurance company also covered my hospital and ambulance bill. Well, most of the bill. We did have to cover the deductible, which was just about the amount of money my mother had saved by hiring Mirta in the first place.

After the accident, two parents pulled their students off the bus. The following year, my mother couldn't find enough new students for the bus and had to relent and let me take the subway to school. That didn't stop her from trying again—she called every Hunter student in Queens to check if their parents also valued money over safety. It was as if my own parents were conspiring against my social standing. My parents were nerds in high school, and they were going to ensure that I was one, too.

"Hey Steve," a student would say as I walked by in the hall. "Your mom called me again this summer. I guess she just can't get enough."

At least they were still calling me Steve.

JUST FOUR DAYS

HUNTER BELIEVES THAT YOU SHOULD SHUFFLE THE DECK
every year, exposing students to the largest possible amount of
new people. That sounds like a great system—except it takes the
little bit of social progress the shyer, quieter kids make each year
and erases it like an Etch A Sketch in an earthquake.

Each year, the quiet kids had to start from scratch and try to
make new friends like we were starting in a new school all over
again. This further cemented the advantage The Clique had over
the rest of us, since The Clique was big enough to always have a
few members in each class.

I didn't have many allies in my new classes, but one of them
was Lindsay Messner. Lindsay was a small, quiet girl who laughed
at my jokes and cracked her own. She didn't like guitars, and she
liked baseball even less. But Lindsay seemed to genuinely enjoy
being around me even if our interests didn't match up. And I
realized I felt the same.

Lindsay wasn't the kind of girl who had most of the grade
pining for her. But she had substance and could relate to me

about one of the most important issues in my life—she knew what it was like to be bullied.

Lindsay was quiet in class and in the halls, but she was talkative around me without issue. It was clear that she was suffering from the same bully-induced, artificial quiet that I was. Lindsay was smart but kept her humor to herself, lest it get her any unnecessary attention. We were perfect for each other. And one day, I realized it.

When you realize you have feelings for someone, the next step is obvious: You keep those feelings to yourself until they boil up inside and destroy you. Or you can act like an adult and tell the person.

After a few weeks of simmering feelings, I did the mature thing and, by passing Lindsay notes in class, let her know I had something important to tell her that I would explain later.

At this point, I was terrified of rejection. Alexa had broken my heart, and Stephanie had rejected me before I had even asked her out. I was hesitant to make myself vulnerable again. You know what they say—fool me once, shame on me. Fool me twice, and it's because I dared to be a quiet kid with a crush on someone of the opposite sex. And please don't fool me three times; I don't know if I could take it.

During lunch, I told Lindsay I had a crush on someone without telling her whom. I was hoping she'd figure it out and either tell me she liked me, too, or tell me that she wasn't interested. That way I could get my answer without ever asking. And if

Lindsay said she wasn't interested, I could pretend that I wasn't either and she had misunderstood. This scheme was the perfect way for a coward to save face.

Lindsay may have figured out I meant her, but she didn't make it easy on me. All she did was ask me who over and over again, until I promised to tell her by passing her notes. I thought this was an excellent strategy. Passing a note in class added an extra element of excitement and danger. Also, I would be smart enough not to put all the information on one note. This would both give Lindsay a chance to say something first if she figured it out and allow me to avoid incrimination if one of the notes fell into the wrong hands. Like Scarlet Daly's hands, for example.

I decided I would pass Lindsay one note per class throughout the afternoon, thus building the suspense. And the annoyance, probably.

My plan was to slowly spell the word Y-O-U on three separate notes. I thought about spelling Lindsay, but by the time I got to the *D*, it'd be pretty obvious. I didn't really think my plan through; after the *O*, Lindsay asked me if I was trying to spell *you*. Of course, the word *you* was even more obvious than the word *Lindsay*. No girl in our school's name started with *Yo*. I don't even think we had a girl in our school whose name started with a *Y*.

It would be hard to mount a convincing defense.

"You think I was trying to spell 'you'? That's ridiculous," I'd say. "I was telling you that I really enjoy the music of classical violinist Yo-Yo Ma. Don't jump to conclusions."

After the O, Lindsay knew how I felt, and I was terrified that she wouldn't return my feelings. Could I take any more rejection? My heart hadn't yet healed from being stomped on by Alexa and being completely ignored by Stephanie. Thankfully Lindsay didn't make me wait long. And that's how I got my second girlfriend.

Lindsay and I sat next to each other during the last class of the day, which was nothing new. I usually sat with Jacob to one side of me and Lindsay to the other, provided we all got to class early enough that there were three desks in a row available. And since we were all nerds, we usually got to class early enough that there were three desks available next to each other.

Since sitting next to each other was something we already did, nothing really changed. And since my note-passing escapade took place on a Friday, Lindsay and I would have to wait until Monday before we were an official school couple. Or maybe not.

That Sunday, one of our classmates, Marley, was having a birthday party. Marley was from a rich family, so this wasn't your average birthday party. Marley had a country home on a huge piece of land about an hour from New York City, and her parents chartered buses to bring the entire grade up there.

I didn't get invited to many parties, so I never missed the few chances that I did have. And this time, I was going with a date. I was going to Marley's party with my new girlfriend.

On the way up to the party, Lindsay had an open seat next to her, so I sat down. I was her boyfriend, after all. This seating arrangement raised eyebrows. Sure, everyone knew Lindsay and I were friends. But why wouldn't I be sitting next to Jacob, annoyingly discussing our favorite guitar players? Something was amiss, and everyone knew it.

I spent the party hanging out with Lindsay. We even went for a romantic walk in the woods. Not too romantic—I had been burned so badly by Alexa that I didn't even have enough courage to hold Lindsay's hand. But Lindsay and I had a pretty great time as platonic boyfriend and girlfriend, and on the bus ride back, I could see everyone was looking at us. We'd been the talk of the party.

On that bus ride, I still didn't have the courage to hold her hand, despite sharing an armrest. But as we watched whatever movie the bus driver put on to shut dozens of teenagers up, I leaned as close to Lindsay as I could without making an actual move. I kept my head at the angle it would be while resting on her shoulder, only without actually touching her. Other classmates were losing their virginity and my big move was a head-tilt. I was a coward, but at least I was a happy coward.

The next day, I was pretty thrilled to get to school. This time when I sat next to Lindsay in class, it'd be different. She wouldn't just be my ally in the fight against the bullies. She'd be my girlfriend. But when I got to class, Lindsay wasn't waiting outside the room like she usually was. I could only save a seat for her so long before someone else grabbed it. Lindsay got to class just before the period started, grabbed an open seat across the room, and took out her notebook. I didn't think much of it—Lindsay was studious and class was starting. She just showed up late. Maybe she missed her bus or walked the long way to class to avoid the bullies. No big deal.

As the day passed, this pattern continued. Lindsay would show up late and grab the open seat across the room or a few rows down and immediately take out her books. I'd occasionally catch her eye from across the room. Lindsay would smile at me but quickly go back to burying her head in her notes. When lunch came, Lindsay told me that she had plans with her girl-friend and asked if it'd be okay if we caught up later. "Sure," I said, realizing that, between the two of us, Lindsay was the only one spending time with a girlfriend.

Meanwhile, the rumor mill was still focused on us. Students I didn't even know stopped me in the hall to ask if Lindsay and I were dating. I told them that we were—in fact, we'd been dating since Friday. This was our fourth day as boyfriend and girlfriend, so it's not like we were brand-new.

Finally, we had a free period before the last class of the day, and Lindsay and I had time to catch up. I was excited to finally spend some quality time with my girlfriend. Too bad I didn't still have one.

Lindsay used that free period to break up with me. Lindsay explained that she couldn't handle the rumors going around about us, that too many people were talking about us, and that she didn't realize the attention that being a couple would bring. She explained that she liked it better when the bullies just ignored her and she couldn't take them speculating on her personal life.

"What's so bad about people paying attention to us?" I asked. I was happy to answer people's questions about us. I certainly preferred this kind of attention to the attention I usually got.

"You don't understand," Lindsay said before leaving me perplexed. She was right. I didn't understand.

Over the next few days, I still didn't understand, but I began to know. The attention I got from our "relationship" was much different than the attention Lindsay got. Lindsay was being called horrible names, most of them some form of or synonym for *slut*. In case you're wondering who started these rumors, you should go back and reread the story about Scarlet Daly.

I tried to tell Lindsay to ignore the idiots, since she and I both knew that we hadn't even held hands, let alone done anything remotely like anyone was saying. But it was too late—people were already spreading wild stories about our walk in the woods, and Lindsay and I were over before we started. Technically we were over four days after we started, but that is pretty much the same thing.

I'd been rejected again, and it was much worse than it would have been if I had been rejected after that second note I passed. I'd gotten my hopes up only to have them dashed. Also, the rumors about us disturbed my sense of justice. I'd have been happier if Lindsay had dumped me because of something I'd done. At least then I could accept it and try to work on improving that part of myself. No, this was a special kind of awful. I felt helpless. I was dumped for something out of my control.

"I like you, Steve," I imagined Lindsay saying. "But the Mets don't look like they'll make the playoffs this year, so I just don't see a future together."

I hated what I was going through, but I also I hated what Lindsay was going through. I wanted to change our fate, but I couldn't. A big romantic gesture would have only made things worse for Lindsay.

Lindsay was right that I didn't understand what she was going through, as I've never been slut-shamed, and I doubt I ever will be. But I did get that the only person in this story who had anything to be ashamed of was Scarlet Daly. I looked forward to the start of the next school year. If there was any justice in the world, when Hunter shuffled the deck again, I'd finally end up in a class free of Scarlet.

BETWEEN THE LINES

IT IS A HARD THING TO REALIZE THAT SOMETIMES dreams are just dreams. I had to finally admit that baseball wasn't my thing.

By the time I was four years old, I was already a baseball fan. I was at a neighbor's house, and they had the Yankee game on. I asked them to change it to the Mets game—because I was raised correctly.

There's a lot to be romantic about when it comes to baseball: the long and recorded history, the lack of a clock, and the timing of starting in the spring. I did love that I could pour through statistics quietly on my own and still be a part of a vast community just by wearing a certain hat. But mainly, I loved baseball because of family.

My father and my brother, David, were baseball fans before I was old enough to understand that Ruth was a man's name. When I was still too young to cross the street, I was playing baseball in a schoolyard with David. Thankfully, we lived on the same block as the school, so no street crossing was necessary.

I signed up for Little League when I was seven, as soon as I was old enough to be eligible. And after getting hits in my first five at bats, I really believed that I was going to be a professional baseball player. Until I got hit in the face.

I was not a brave kid. Hell, I'm not a brave adult. But as a kid, I was terrified of pain. Theo eventually used this very fear to torture me. No one explained to me that pain is temporary. No one explained to me that the vast majority of injuries a kid sustains go away as soon as that kid sees ice cream. I was always scared of getting hurt, and then one day I did.

The pitch wasn't coming fast. We were young enough that our coaches were the ones pitching to us, and maybe that's why I didn't get out of the way in time—I had no reason to suspect that my coach would hit me in the damn face. I don't even know how it happened. I was seven. I had a small face.

After I got beaned, I was a different player. Despite going five for my first five, I didn't get a hit again the rest of that season. I was afraid to face any pitcher, even my coach.

I could no longer hit, but I was a solid fielder, and years of playing catch with my older brother meant I had a good arm. I started teaching myself to pitch. Pitchers aren't expected to be good hitters. And maybe if I worked hard enough at it, *I* could be the one who accidentally hit people in the face.

I wasn't a very good pitcher—I didn't know how to grip the

ball correctly or how to have the right form. I just knew you're supposed to aim it over the plate and throw as hard as you can. It turns out there's a bit more nuance than that.

When Hunter fielded a junior varsity baseball team for the first time, I signed up immediately. Our coach had no experience at all—he was an assistant science teacher who had barely ever held a baseball glove. But somehow he ended up in charge of a bunch of students pretending to be a baseball team. Our first game was so messy, it was like a pick-up game with one adult watching. I watched, too—I was a pitcher, after all. Pitchers don't get to play in every game.

After that game, it was my coach's lack of experience that led him to say one of the dumbest things I've ever heard someone say. "Steve—you're starting against Horace Mann."

Horace Mann was a prep school with one of the best baseball teams in the city. And I, the worst pitcher on the worst team in the city, was going to be starting against them. My coach was sending me on a suicide mission.

Somehow, I got the first batter to ground out. The second reached on a single and I walked the third. And then, the fourth batter grounded my first pitch right to our second baseman, who fielded it cleanly and started a double play that ended the inning. Sorry—that's what should have happened. Instead, the ball bounced off his glove, everyone was safe, and the inning continued for a very, very long time.

Many hits and errors later (including another one by the

second baseman), I'd given up eight runs. If I'd died on the mound, we'd have forfeited. A forfeit is scored as a 9–0 loss. My performance was only one run better than an actual suicide mission.

I had lost any composure I pretended to have. I wasn't just hittable now; I was wild. I was trying to throw my arm off, doing anything I could to just get out of that damn inning. That's when I let a ball get away from me. And I hit someone.

I didn't hit him in the face, but I flashed back to getting hit as a child anyway. That paired with my horrible inning (or third of an inning) left me rattled. It was clear to anyone watching that I was done. My inexperienced coach mercifully yanked me. We joined the league late, so this was the last game of the season; I don't know why he left me in so long. It's not like we were saving our other pitchers for the playoffs. Put as many people in as you need to in order to end this carnage, and let us go get ice cream.

My coach didn't remove me completely; he pulled a double switch and left me in as the designated hitter. Hitter? Really? That's the thing I was worst at. For a science teacher, my coach was pretty allergic to facts. I never had him as a science teacher, and I'm glad. I wouldn't want to learn that the atomic weight of tungsten is whatevs.

Even if I had been a good hitter, I now had to get back into a solid headspace by the time I was at bat. When the top of that inning finally ended, my team poured back into the dugout. Most of them ignored me or gave me an encouraging pat on the shoulder. But one of them didn't see the importance of helping my headspace and chose to yell at me instead.

Of all people to tell me how much I sucked, how I ruined everything, and how I had no business playing baseball, it was our second baseman. The same second baseman whose errors started this mess. The same second baseman who had been torturing me all year. The same second baseman who was named Theo Webster.

I grabbed a bat out of the bat rack and started toward Theo; I was angry and I wanted to scare him. I had no intention of actually hitting Theo, but even threatening him was stupid. Standing up to Theo was the right thing to do, but sans Louisville Slugger. Or whatever knock-off bat our team could afford.

Grabbing that bat was a weak, emotional moment, and it takes a stronger person to not fight than it does to fight. And several even stronger people got between me and Theo. My coach did the only smart thing he did all season and finally took me out of the game.

When I got home, I was inconsolable. I was upset at how I had pitched and upset at how I had reacted to Theo and upset at the reality that baseball was not going to be my ticket to a scholarship. As much as I loved watching the game, I wasn't going to be playing it.

I asked my brother, who was as big of a baseball fan as I was and whose baseball career was just as over as mine, what to do next. And my brother gave me the advice that would change my life.

David drew three parallel lines on a piece of paper.

"Most people," he said, pointing to the middle line, "live their life here. They don't go far down, but they don't go far up either. The further you go toward this top line, the further you will also go toward this bottom line. You decide if that's worth it. I've never been a fan of the middle."

It was a tough day for me, but he was right. I'd much rather have highs and lows than a bunch of middles. Sure, I'd never play professional baseball. But that is true of almost everyone in the world.

One other thing that made me feel better was the realization that because of the errors, all the runs I gave up were unearned. I finished my baseball career with a pristine 0.00 ERA. That's a Hall of Fame number.

IMPROV-MENT

AFTER THE DEBACLES OF ALEXA HOWARD, STEPHANIE
Spencer, and Lindsay Messner, it would have made sense for me
to try to avoid any attempts at romantic entanglements for a
while. But the heart wants what it wants. Also, Elaine Audley,
my new crush, was very, very pretty.

Elaine's smile aside, I didn't let my mistakes determine who I
was. As long as you learn something from a mistake, it's not truly
a mistake. If you cross the street and get hit by a car, the lesson
is not to avoid crossing the street again. It's to cross the street
more carefully. And to not cross it with Alexa Howard lest you
get pushed into traffic.

The lesson I learned from dating Alexa was that some people
will be more interested in the *idea* of dating you than actually
dating you. The lesson I learned from pining for Stephanie is that
simply being attracted to someone isn't enough to make a connection. The lesson I learned from trying to date Lindsay was to
not let what other people say about your actions dictate those
actions.

Elaine had been a child model who grew up to be a teen model. Beyond being beautiful, she was also extremely kind to me. Unlike Alexa, who was nice enough until she wasn't anymore, Elaine was genuinely interested in me as a person. She went out of her way to say hello to me, always asked how I was, and smiled directly at me rather than simply in my general direction.

I don't remember the pretext I used the first time I called Elaine. It was probably about a homework assignment or another equally transparent excuse.

If I was being honest, the conversation would have opened like this: "Hi, Elaine? This is Steve. I just wanted to ask you a question I could have asked literally any other person in our class. But while I have you on the line . . ."

The only time such a ruse works is when the other person wants you to call them anyway. By the third week of school, everyone (even the quiet redhead) had plenty of people they could call about homework. When you call someone outside of your circle, there's clearly an ulterior motive.

Once, I was almost at the receiving end of one of those calls. When I was a junior in high school, I came home from Jacob's apartment and my mother let me know that "some girl called asking about the physics homework."

"Who was it?" I asked, impatient. My mother didn't remember the girl's name. I freaked out, and my mother couldn't understand why. There was a pretty obvious explanation for why I was so upset: I had never taken physics. This was a girl calling me with the same type of weak excuse I'd used for years, and my mother hadn't bothered to remember who it was. The physics girl never called back, probably assuming I'd received the message and taking my failure to respond as rejection. I agonized, trying to find out who that girl was. Thanks, Mom.

But my homework ruse worked with Elaine, and we started talking often. Often soon turned into every day. After school, we'd sit on the phone for hours, talking about nearly everything. Everything but the fact that I clearly liked her.

Did Elaine know? She couldn't have. If she knew I liked her and she liked me back, she'd have said something. And if she knew I liked her and she didn't like me, we wouldn't have been talking this much. I must have been doing a wonderful job of hiding my feelings by calling her every single day.

After two months of this, I finally asked Elaine to lunch.

"Wow!" you might be saying. "Where did Steve suddenly get the courage to ask a model on a date?"

Simple. I didn't.

I asked Elaine to go to lunch with me, and as silence enveloped the world, I threw in, "as friends." I chickened out like I was being served in the cafeteria.

As friends was a technique taught to me by one of my new friends, Rebecca Chaikin (a girl I was actually just friends with). Rebecca was the first platonic female friend I'd had, and she was extremely valuable—Rebecca often shared her insights into female behavior. Like the as-friends gambit.

The idea was simple: Ask a girl to lunch and make it clear that you're just asking as a friend. Guy friends eat lunch together all the time, right? That way the girl won't feel any pressure to say yes, the guy won't be rejected, and you'll both get some quality alone time together. Once you're on the non-date, she'll be so charmed by your winsome personality that you'll be in a relationship before you know it!

This was, and is, a horrible idea.

I was voluntarily banishing myself to the friend zone. Rebecca was a dear friend, but she knew just as little about picking up women as I did. You can't trick someone into being attracted to you by simply spending platonic time near them. And Elaine was not attracted to me. Thankfully, Elaine spared me the indignity of going to a platonic lunch by turning me down, even as friends. Perhaps she saw through my homework ruse after all.

Elaine and I still talked, as she really did value me as a friend—she just didn't want to lead me on. Our phone conversations stayed just as frequent, and during one of them, Elaine told me about how she'd joined the improv club and how much fun it was.

That was the best thing about Hunter: The school was known for its academics—but the clubs! There was a radio club, a skateboarding club, and even an LGBT club. That may not seem like a big deal now, but in the early 1990s, that was not common. Hunter had a club that catered to every aspect of every lifestyle, hobby, and pursuit, no matter how trivial. There was also a board game club where they probably played Trivial Pursuit.

I didn't know anything about improv, but I knew a ton about stand-up comedy. In addition to the George Carlin albums my father raised me on, I consumed every bit of stand-up I could find. My favorite show was "Comic Strip Live," and I even enjoyed Andrew Dice Clay and Dennis Leary. As I told you, I was derivative back then.

A few years earlier, I had written some ideas for jokes, mainly because my brother had done the same. But I never had any intention of performing them. I was too shy and too quiet. Those jokes were just written for me.

Improv terrified me. I was a writer; I wasn't funny off-the-cuff. Despite the success of my "Steve, please!" opener, I'd bombed ever since. Improv sounded like one of the toughest things a person could do, other than continue to go to school surrounded by bullies.

None of my fears mattered when Elaine told me I should join the improv club. We may not have been going to lunch together, but I still liked and respected her. When Elaine told me to do anything, I said yes.

Elaine didn't *just* tell me I should join the improv club. Elaine told me I should join the improv club because I was funny. What? Elaine Audley thought I was funny? Maybe all those hours on the phone had paid off.

No one thought I was funny. I didn't even think I was funny

anymore. Okay, Elaine, I'm in. Can I join immediately? When do they meet? Do you think they'd mind if I waited in the hallway for the next three days until they do? Where is this bridge I'm supposed to jump from?

The improv club met in a classroom every Monday during lunch. For an hour, two-dozen teenagers played classic improv games like Party Quirks, Quotes, and World's Worst. It wasn't groundbreaking comedy, but it was groundbreaking for me. To see people my own age creating like this was something I didn't think was possible. I was enthralled from the first game.

Students of varying ages were generating comedy out of nothing, and they all seemed to respect one another. There were no bullies here—only people who valued one another as much as they valued getting a laugh. Because improv is not a solo art, you need to be adept at teamwork in order to excel. There were no Tommys or Theos here. Bullies like Tommy and Theo would fall flat on their faces in the improv club. Which would actually be pretty funny.

Something Elaine didn't tell me was that the improv club had a tradition of forcing first-time attendees to perform. It may have been a trial by fire to see if you have the confidence and courage for improv, or it may have been just the world's softest hazing ritual. But, like I'd been doing in class since I got to Hunter, I slumped in my chair and tried not to be noticed.

When Sheryl, the president of the improv club, realized I hadn't performed yet, she called my name. Reluctantly, I walked to the "stage"—the area of the room where the teacher's desk usually resided—and proceeded to play a game of Questions.

The way questions works is two people create a scene by alternating asking questions. The goal is to build on what the last person said and to construct comedy from creatively staying within the limits of the game. The participants are told who they are and what the scene is, like someone getting pulled over for speeding. And the rest is up to them.

I was told to start. "What seems to be the problem, officer?"—a meek cliché.

The other participant countered. "Do you know how fast you were going?"

"Why, is your radar gun broken?" I asked, getting a mild chuckle.

"Have you been drinking?"

"Have *you* been drinking?" My first solid laugh.

"Could you please step out of the car?"

"Are you asking if you can borrow my car?" Boom.

"Do you have a good lawyer?"

And onward, until someone breaks. It's fast-paced with a ton of room to build comedy, and I took to it immediately. I was getting laughs. Not "Steve, please" laughs, but real laughs. The kind of laughs I'd grown up watching stand-up comedians get. The years I'd spent making up stories with my sister Beth had prepared me for this.

For the first time, I saw hope of being truly good at something.

I was a decent card player. I was adequate at guitar. I even had just enough hand-eye coordination to be a passable athlete (though not a decent pitcher). This was different. Improv was mine from word one.

After the scene, the club dispersed and I rushed over to talk to Sheryl. I had so many questions. Did I do it right? Was there anything I could improve on? Is there any good way to practice at home? Was there a resource I could study between now and next week? How do I make sure I get chosen for more scenes in the future? Sheryl answered as much as she could and then politely told me she had to get to class and she'd see me next Monday.

Because my mind and mouth were racing, I didn't notice that the rest of the club had gone. I was so filled with adrenaline, I wasn't thinking about Elaine. Elaine had been the entire reason I went to that club, but in the excitement, I'd forgotten about her. It turned out I liked improv way more than I liked Elaine Audley.

I ran through the halls and got to my next class just in time. The seats near Elaine were already taken, so I grabbed the last empty chair on the other side of the room, gave Elaine a smile, and pulled out my notebook.

Elaine and I had gone to lunch as friends after all. And I'd had a wonderful time.

FEAT

URE

LOOK AT THIS GIANT KINNUS

UNITED SYNAGOGUE YOUTH (OR USY AS IT'S COMMONLY
called) is an international organization for Jewish kids in high
school. There are about three hundred chapters around North
America with a membership of about fifteen thousand kids
total. While I was the first Hofstetter to go to Hunter, I was
a legacy in USY. My parents were very active in our synagogue—that was their social life, and it was expected to be
ours as well. My siblings had all been USY members before
me. I don't recall my mother ever asking me if I wanted to join
USY. It was more her telling me when we were leaving to go
there.

Unlike high school, a youth group is a self-selecting crowd
because it's a nerdy activity. You're not going to find many hooligans meeting every Wednesday night to make potato latkes and
Puffy Paint shirts with motivational phrases. We were at Hunter
because we had to be. No matter how much anyone enjoyed their

extracurricular activities or valued what they learned in class, we went to high school because the state gave us no choice.

When it came to USY, my mother was my personal truancy officer. We were all there because we chose to be or because our parents chose it for us. Either way, there were no hooligans—if hooligans listened to their parents, they wouldn't be hooligans. Maybe rapscallions or no-goodniks, but certainly not hooligans.

A few weekends each year, USY has something called a Kinnus. *Kinnus* is a Hebrew word for gathering. But it also rhymes with penis and I found that hilarious. I didn't go to the first one that year—there was a registration fee, so I didn't even bother to ask my parents. Also, I was intimidated by the idea of socializing for an entire weekend. An hour on a Wednesday, that I could handle. But for an introvert, a whole weekend was overwhelming.

As the second Kinnus approached, my chapter advisor asked me if I was going. I told her I couldn't: there was a registration fee, and my parents didn't have the money. That was an excuse that no person in authority would challenge without risking sounding like an asshole.

My advisor responded that two members from our chapter got to go for free, and she offered me one of the spots. She was not an asshole.

The thought of representing the chapter overwhelmed me even more than simply attending. What a responsibility! Was I worthy of such an honor? What if I embarrassed everyone?

This kind of thing should go to the chapter president and vice president, not me.

My advisor then elaborated: No one else was able to go, and she *needed* someone to represent the chapter. Oh—so this wasn't an honor at all. This was a desperate plea from my advisor. That, I could handle.

"What goes on there? What do people do all weekend?" I asked.

"Well, you'd stay in someone's house," she replied. "Volunteers from the community house the members, and they make sure you get back and forth to all the events."

So you sleep on some dingy floor? I assumed, given the general scarcity of beds in my own home. Maybe not even a floor. Maybe I'd have to sleep on a bolt of denim. *Sounds terrible.*

"It's usually people who have extra rooms to put you up, so the more well-off members of the community."

Big rich houses? Without stuff all over them? I perked up. *Okay, I'm listening.*

"Friday night, there's a big dinner," my advisor went on. "Usually there's an icebreaker of some sort so you can meet people. They try to make sure that the guys and the girls are interacting."

Girls who are forced to talk to me? Go on. This scenario was getting better and better.

Finally, she clinched the deal. "Then Saturday there's an

activity," she said. "It's cold out, so you'll probably do something indoors, like a discussion group or a talent show."

I asked my advisor to clarify if I might be able to do improv at this talent show.

"Sure. I don't see why not."

I was in.

I took the registration materials home that night and asked my mother to fill them out and send them in. When I arrived at the meeting the following week, I excitedly told my advisor that everything was all set.

"Are you sure?" she asked. "I talked to them yesterday and they said they didn't have anything from you."

When my mother picked me up after the meeting, I begged her to tell me that my advisor was wrong and that everything was in place for me to do improv in front of girls. I didn't phrase it that way out loud, I promise.

My mother told me that she hadn't sent in the forms yet, and she didn't understand why I was in such a hurry since the event wasn't for another two weeks. I tried to explain that the whole point of having the registration forms was the ability to register ahead of time. I kept it to myself that she may have ruined my chance to do improv in front of girls.

Growing up, my parents' lack of urgency was a common theme. I assume it's difficult to raise four children, especially four children with mouths like ours. But my parents were late for everything. I once got to a Little League playoff game an hour after it started, which is two hours after we were asked to get there. And the game was only ten minutes from my house. When I learned the term *fashionably late*, I remarked that my parents must be the most fashionable people in the world. If a rapper had asked my parents, "y'all ready for this?" they would have needed another hour to answer.

I finally got my mother to send in the form, and I called daily for the next three days to make sure it arrived and was processed. When I finally got confirmation that the form was in, I was told I was on the waiting list. The event had already filled up.

That was it. My dreams of impressing strange girls with my newfound comedy skills were gone. And then, something incredible happened.

There hadn't been much snow that winter in New York City. Rain, sleet, ice, sure—but no snow. That Tuesday, it started snowing and it didn't stop. The predicted two inches became four and then six and then ten. The city completely shut down in a way New York rarely does. And when the storm finally subsided, a new deluge hit the northeast less than twenty-four hours later. I was so wrapped up in not having to go to school that week that I didn't even think of the ramifications that a historically bad blizzard would have on the Kinnus.

Due to the snow, the Kinnus had to be postponed until two weeks later. And, because some of the previously registered members couldn't attend on the rescheduled date, I was bumped up from the waiting list.

The weekend was everything I'd hoped for. Everyone was friendly. There were no bullies. I didn't have to be quiet there; people introduced themselves to me instead of just walking by. Since everyone had already met the rest of the freshmen at the first Kinnus, they actually seemed excited to meet the mysterious new redhead.

When the advisors announced the surprise event, it was not a talent show. It was an improv show from Second City. Had this been a movie, the script would have been rejected for being too unbelievable. But there was no script. This was improv.

When Second City took volunteers for a game, I ripped my arm off my shoulder and threw it at the improvisers with my remaining hand. At least, that is the force and speed with which I volunteered. They called on me, and I used everything I'd learned in the improv club to own that scene like my mom owned a bolt of denim.

The scene was a doctor's office, and it opened with one of the improvisers portraying a patient complaining that they were homesick.

"Yes, and," I replied, drawing on my training. "How long have you been sick of being home?"

The improviser built off my idea and told me that the problem is they come from a big family and can never get any privacy.

"I know how that is," I said, miming writing on a clip board. "My family is enormous. Seven mothers and three dads."

"Now take this cup," I continued, "and go in the other room and give me a semen sample."

There was a shocked murmer in the crowd. This was a religious youth group, and I was up there doing a dick joke.

"How will that help cure my homesickness?" The improviser responded, caught off guard by me going dirty and trying to get the scene back on track.

"It won't," I countered. "But you have a big family. It's probably your only chance."

The crowd went crazy, and the improviser said, "Goodnight, everybody!" Maybe he wanted to end on a laugh, or maybe he was preventing the scene from getting bluer. I was happy it was over without a misstep. Unlike when I played baseball, I was three for three. I walked back to my seat no longer the mysterious new redhead. Now everyone knew me as the funny kid.

After that, my insecurity vanished, at least at my USY meetings. Hunter was the same as it had been before USY. I was still quiet there, outside of the improv club. I went to class, played guitar with Jacob, and talked baseball if the subject came up. But I kept my secret youth group life to myself. Over the next few months, I went to every USY event I could. I didn't care if it was a Kinnus or a boat ride or a meeting or a dance. I went. I boated. I danced. It turns out that years of playing guitar in your room by yourself can give you rhythm. Objectively, I wasn't a great dancer. But in a room full of Jewish teenagers, I was Beyoncé. That is a strange sentence to write, but you get the idea.

By the end of the year, I'd made friends, including a close friend named Mason who came with me to every event. I don't remember how I became friends with Mason because it was so instant and effortless. One day we had never met each other, then suddenly we were talking about baseball and stand-up and which event we'd go to next. Some people you just vibe with.

With my newfound feeling of belonging, I did what I never thought I'd do—I entered a popularity contest. I decided to run for vice president of my USY chapter. If I was going to be the dancing funny kid, I should at least have a formal title. I made sure to get the paperwork in the first day I could—I wasn't going to be waitlisted for this one.

The thought of losing worried me because I still feared rejection. I remembered my brother's advice and how I'd have to risk losing in order to win. I figured if I lost to whichever challenger might come forward, at least I'd have tried. And then no one else came forward.

Every other position was contested except for mine. The other members running for office assumed I couldn't be beat and decided they were better off not trying. I didn't just win—the rest of the chapter forfeited. This wasn't a huge victory; my chapter only had about twenty members. But I could not have imagined wanting a leadership position even a year prior, let alone winning one uncontested.

I often think about how much that snowstorm changed my life. And not just because it gave me a few days off from school.

THE MARVELOUS INTERNSHIP

ONE DAY, AS I CONTINUED MY TRADITION OF WALKING through Hunter's halls silently, an opportunity for change presented itself. I found seventy-five cents in one of the stairwells. But I mean change in the other sense, too.

I picked up the quarters, put them in my pocket, and walked downstairs to get lunch. As I got to the basement, a younger student approached me.

"Would you like to buy some comic books?" he asked someone who'd never bought a comic book.

"No thanks," I said. "Not my thing."

It is strange that I wasn't into comic books, as I was the target audience. I was nerdy, I loved to read, and most of all, I enjoyed escapism. A world where heroes always won should have been pretty appealing to someone frustrated by defeat. But comic books cost money, and I didn't have money.

"Come on. I'm selling them for just twenty-five cents each."

I thought about the change in my pocket and saw that the cover price on each of the comics was well more than twenty-five cents each. These weren't just comic books—these were heavily discounted comic books. This was an investment.

I don't know why the kid was selling them for pennies on the dollar. But I'd just found seventy-five cents, and I could turn that into three shiny new comic books. If I'd found three comic books, I'd probably have been happier than if I'd found seventy-five cents. So I bought them, and my appreciation for all things Marvel began.

Before those books, the only superhero I cared much about was Batman. I'd always liked Batman because he had no super-powers. Sure, he had unlimited wealth, but when you get down to it, Batman was a superhero because he wanted to be one and he put the work in.

Over the next few months, I fell in love with superheroes. I babysat every weekend to make enough money to buy as many comic books as I could. I became obsessed with popular stalwarts like the X-Men and Spider-Man, found more esoteric heroes like Darkhawk, and even got into the super-cheesy Captain America.

I loved the teamwork of the X-Men, that Spider-Man was a dork (and Mary Jane was a redhead!), that Darkhawk was a troubled teenager who didn't fit in, and that Captain America had a tremendous sense of what was right. I dreamed of waking up and learning I was a mutant, and I tried to figure out what power would be best to defeat Tommy and Theo. Super-strength is the obvious choice, but tossing a web over their mouths was also a wonderful idea.

I developed strong opinions on who was the best Silver Surfer artist (Ron Lim) and which was the most pointless superhero team (Alpha Flight). And I started drawing (poorly). A world where heroes always won *was* pretty appealing to me after all.

I should have found this years prior. Some of my fellow Freak Hallway-ers were artists and welcomed me as I learned to be one of them. I wasn't a very good artist, though I got better as I practiced. My fellow freaks taught me techniques like cross-hatching and stippling and laughed with me at my mistakes instead of mocking me. But no matter how good I got, looking at the work of my classmates let me know how good I wasn't by comparison.

These kids were truly talented artists. It occurred to me that they had spent their years of not fitting in learning how to express themselves non-verbally, while I wasted mine worrying about not fitting in. Some of their work was just stunning. My work, on the other hand, was okay for someone who'd never drawn anything before.

A senior named Ciro petitioned Hunter to let him start a comic book club that would meet once a week. And at the end of the semester, the club planned to print its own comic book. By comic book, I mean "photocopied black-and-white cheap-looking thing with some clever stories in it."

I was interested immediately. I'd learned to be more confident in my creativity through improv, and I'd learned how to make friends through USY. Working on that comic book was a combination of the two.

One day after school, Ciro had an idea. "Why don't we take the subway to Marvel?"

Could we do that? Sure, anyone who owned any comic book Marvel ever published knew their address. It was right there in the front of each book: 387 Park Avenue South. Door to door, Marvel was less than twenty minutes by subway. I was in.

I wondered what we would do when we got there. Was Marvel open to the public? Did they have a museum and gift shop with lots of wonderful things I couldn't afford? Were there people dressed like superheroes everywhere? Did Ron Lim have an office just twenty minutes from my high school?

As we approached the Marvel building, I got nervous. Luckily, we were able to get inside without buzzing by, sidling in as someone else was sidling out. I'm sure we fit right in—two pimply, overexcited boys with backpacks. Given that Marvel is a comic book company, we probably did fit in.

Quickly, my anxiety was replaced by a feeling of overwhelming awe. The lobby had framed prints of classic covers and a rack with the new issue of just about every title—including ones that hadn't even hit stores yet.

"Can I help you?" The woman at the front desk broke through our bewildered haze.

"Yes, thank you," I said, my improv training kicking in. "Our school has an internship program, and we were wondering if you had any positions open for the spring semester."

This ruse worked way better than *as friends* had. The woman at the desk said that she'd be happy to pass on the information about their program to the internship coordinator. Then she offered us a tour.

The obvious answer was *yes*. Or, as far as suddenly silent Ciro was concerned, a bewildered nod.

There wasn't a ton to see—it was an office, after all. But we were led around the cubicles for about fifteen minutes and taught about the production process, and we got to see some unfinished pages and recognized many names on many doors. When it was all over, our host gave me the phone number for the internship coordinator and walked us out.

As we were leaving, the receptionist pointed to the rack with the new issues on it and said, "Why don't you take a few souvenirs?"

Ciro hadn't spoken a word the entire tour, but now I fell silent, too.

"Go ahead," she said. "That's why they're there. Take whatever you'd like."

I grabbed *X-Men*, *Spider-Man*, *Silver Surfer*, *Darkhawk*, and *Captain America*. I didn't want to be greedy, so I just grabbed the books I would have bought anyway. Ciro was too petrified to move, so I grabbed a few more and shoved them in his hand.

It took me two weeks to muster up the courage to call the

internship coordinator. And when I did, a very nice woman named Mary picked up. Mary told me that the receptionist had filled her in on our visit, and she was surprised I hadn't called yet. While I contemplated a viable excuse, Mary launched into the description of the internship program. And then she asked what college I went to.

"I'm in high school," I responded, crestfallen.

"Oh," Mary said. "Well, that's unusual. And your high school has an internship program?"

"Kind of," I said, immediately regretting my informality and quickly switching to a more professional vocabulary. "They encourage us to pursue extracurricular opportunities beyond the classroom."

"You mean they want you to get after-school jobs."

I paused to try to come up with an impressive answer. I did not have one.

"Yes."

Hunter did have an internship program, but it was only for seniors. And even Ciro wouldn't be eligible because he already had an internship at his father's law firm. There were probably no free comic books there.

Mary explained to me that she couldn't arrange anything for after school, because their day would be close to done by the time I got there. But if I could come for a half day each week, they could find something for me.

Marvel freaking Comics had just offered me an internship. But first, I had a few hurdles to clear.

I told my mother. Well, the words fell out of my mouth in front of my mother. She gave me permission if my teachers were okay with me missing the time.

I figured out that Thursdays would work for Mary's one-day-a-week mandate. I had only two afternoon classes—English and Math. They were the only two classes where I was doing well, and the teachers liked me. Both teachers said yes. Second hurdle cleared. But the final hurdle was tougher to defeat than Magneto, the Green Goblin, Thanos, Lodestone, and the Red Skull combined. The final hurdle was my principal, Dr. Haanraats.

Dr. Haanraats was a tall, thin, unflappable man who had been the principal of the high school since the dawn of time. There was an easy-to-believe rumor that he lived across the street from Hunter and jogged around it at five A.M. just to keep an eye on the place. In order to accept Marvel's internship, my teachers said I needed his blessing.

I quietly and carefully walked into his office like I was Captain America looking for stolen World War II paintings. I asked if Dr. Haanraats was available. Much to my chagrin, he was. I was led into Dr. Haanraats's office and encouraged to have a seat across from him. I would rather have been looking for World War II paintings.

I told Dr. Haanraats about the internship, how Mary said that I was the youngest student Marvel had ever offered it to, and how much it would mean to me. I told him that I had my teachers' blessings. I told him about my typically strict mother somehow green-lighting this. And I asked him if he could be the final sign-off.

Dr. Haanraats gave a brief and cold "no."

My timidity was immediately replaced by anger. I wanted to scream at him. I wanted to flip his desk over. But my improv training prevailed.

"Hunter is a good high school, isn't it?" I asked rhetorically. He gave me a confused "yes" in reply.

"Well," I continued. "The point of going to a good high school is to work hard and get accepted to a good college. And the point of going to a good college is to work hard and get a good job. And here I am, being offered a good job. So, shouldn't we take it?"

I felt clever. I even included him in the *we* so that this could be his success, too. I also felt proud that I wasn't taking no for an answer. This wasn't like when I stood up to Alexa or when I tried to stand up to Scarlet. This was so much more important. Unfortunately, my efforts were useless.

"My answer is final," Dr. Haanraats said. "I take my students' education very seriously, and I do not let them skip school to play with comic books."

Play with comic books. Now I understood. If this were an internship at a hospital or on the floor of the stock market or at Ciro's father's law firm, Dr. Haanraats would have taken it seriously. But to him, this was childish. To him, Rembrandt was an artist. Ron Lim, who I am sure Dr. Haanraats had never heard of, was a clown with a pen.

"It is a shame you didn't have an opportunity like this when you were my age," I snapped as I stormed out. "Maybe you wouldn't have ended up a high school principal."

Thankfully, I was out of the room before Dr. Haanraats could react. I knew I'd let my anger get the best of me. I also knew that being a high school principal was a fine and respectable job. But sometimes in improv the scene takes over.

STAY TOGETHER FOR THE KIDS

MUCH LIKE ROMEO AND JULIET, MY PARENTS DREW closer together because their families tried to keep them apart. But Romeo and Juliet had the good sense to end things before they brought kids into it.

I cannot remember a time in my life when my parents weren't fighting. When I was a toddler, the fights would end in extended make-up hugs. Toddler Steve thought it was funny to crawl between their legs to try to push them apart as they hugged. Maybe I knew that the peace between my parents, like the hug, was only temporary.

As my siblings and I got older, the fighting got worse and the hugs vanished. My parents were never physically harmful to each other, but they yelled and they screamed and they cried. Oh boy, did they cry. My house was like someone chopping onions during a Sarah McLachlan animal-adoption ad.

The fighting didn't bother the kids too much, and we did what we always did: We responded with humor. On one of David's birthdays, my mother was screaming at him to do the dishes. As he ignored her, she stormed into the dining room and said, "You will do those dishes, birthday or no birthday." I replied, "birthday."

But David had the best comeback of our entire childhood. My father, after a particularly rough back-and-forth, screamed at David to "go to hell." David calmly replied, "Maybe we can carpool."

I was twelve when my parents sat us all down to announce a working separation where my mother would move into the basement but my parents would stay married. If you've never heard of a working separation where one parent lives in the basement before, that's because it's a ridiculous idea. Sometimes I wonder what life would have been like if I had grown up in Los Angeles, where there are no basements.

Our basement was not a place where someone could physically sleep, let alone work on their marriage. My mother cleared out some boxes of wrapping paper, a filing cabinet, and whatever other garbage was in the way to make room for a bed. As she cleaned, she discovered there was already a bed down there, just buried under some boxes of wrapping paper, a filing cabinet, and whatever other garbage was in the way. The bolt of denim stayed put, since it lived in the dining room.

My parents' separation lasted only a few months before my mother moved back upstairs. Did that mean that my parents had worked through their separation? According to the fighting, no. It was more likely that my mother was tired of sleeping amid filing cabinets.

I'd imagined she filed all of her emotions down there: "This drawer is A through E. It's where I file all my anger, angst, anxiety, bitterness, blame, chagrin, codependence, conflict, confusion, contempt, despair, disappointment, drama, and ennui. I have a separate drawer for F."

Two years later, my parents finally announced the divorce we all saw coming. A battle over property ensued and lasted particularly long because both of my parents were pack rats. My parents argued over every little thing—even old, frayed towels that neither of them had used in years. One thing I learned from my parents' divorce was that you shouldn't marry anyone you couldn't handle getting divorced from. It seems antithetical, but if you'd ever watched two people arguing over an old, frayed towel, you'd understand.

It had become painfully clear that for the last few years of their marriage that my parents had been staying together for the kids. In their case, that idea was dumber than the working separation. If someone is contemplating divorce and doesn't go through with it because they're afraid they won't see their kids, I get that. But to prolong a toxic environment as if that will somehow be better for the development of children is ridiculous. I love both of my parents, but my home life got much better after their divorce.

The next step after dividing up the things that didn't matter was to divide up the things that did. Since most of what my parents owned was worthless, I'm certainly not talking about any family heirlooms or Swiss bank accounts. After the frayed towels, it was time to divide up the kids.

I have three siblings, but my oldest sister, Leah, was already engaged and on her way out of the house at the time so it was just me, Beth, and David. My parents, for all their fighting and ridiculousness, both loved us very much and both wanted all three of us. Since they couldn't make a decision, they let us choose. I realize that I am lucky to have been raised by two parents who both wanted to keep their children. But I was not lucky to have been the mediator.

I've made clear throughout this book that I had problems with my parents' lateness, their frugality, and their seemingly hereditary nerd-dom. But I loved them both, and choosing which one to live with was as difficult as getting to a Little League game on time. Picking which parent to live with was the toughest decision I've made in my life. I imagine it was slightly tougher than negotiating which ratty towel to keep.

The first part of the decision was easy. David, Beth, and I wanted to stay together. So we concluded that our decision had to be unanimous. And as real estate agents say, the remaining choice came down to location, location, location.

My mother's plan was to move to Forest Hills, a neighborhood in central Queens convenient to Manhattan, with a ton of subway access. Meanwhile, my father was moving to Bellerose, a neighborhood with no subway at all that is as far east as you can go and still be considered in New York City. Bellerose is in New York City like Attu Station, Alaska, is in the United States.

If we lived with my mother, Beth could leave the school she hated and be zoned for one of the best public high schools in New York. David would be just two miles from his college campus. And I would have a forty-five-minute commute to Hunter instead of the 90-minute commute I'd have with my father. The answer was not easy, but it was obvious.

When we told each of them our choice of who we were going to live with, we wanted to make sure they understood exactly what they had put us through. So, after we let them know we'd decided on our mother, we asked each parent to choose which one of the kids they'd live with if they could also only choose one.

My father paused, smiled, and gave us a "touché." He was proud of us not only for having the emotional maturity to understand the gravity of the question but also for having the dark sense of humor to spin the decision on him. My father thought for a bit and chose me. I was the most easygoing of the three kids and thus the easiest to live with. It made sense—I'd spent my time at Hunter learning how to not be in the way. Besides, he'd previously told David to go to hell.

My mother had a different reaction. She burst into tears, said she realized what a horrible thing we had had to go through, and *blah blah* more crying *blah*. It was the Sarah McLachlan onions all over again. Sure, my siblings and I had made our point, but we were tired of tears—we would rather have gotten an answer and my mother had gotten the joke.

Before David, Beth, and I were done, there was one more joke we needed to tell, and this time we were guaranteed laughs—we were our own audience.

The reason I haven't written much about my sister Leah is that she is six years older than me and she wasn't really part of the immature hijinks that bonded the rest of us. David, Beth, and I stayed up late watching stand-up while Leah stayed up late to tell us to go to bed. The best description of her came from David, who commented, "she's at the age where she should be having fun instead of telling other people not to." At the time David described her that way, Leah was a teenager and genuinely excited to pick out wallpaper.

Beth, David, and I gathered in Leah's room and gave her our fictional news. We weren't choosing our mother or father— we were choosing her. In an Oscar-worthy performance, the three of us convinced Leah that, because she'd looked out for us all these years, we thought that her and her new husband would be the best option for us. We somehow kept our faces straight as Leah's face contorted, trying to hide her panic. As

THE TEACHER WHO TAUGHT ME EVERYTHING

THE FIRST FEW DAYS OF TENTH GRADE WERE PARTICU-larly difficult. We had moved to Forest Hills after the divorce, and the first night in the new apartment was my birthday. Moving isn't easy on anyone. But coupling moving with your parents' divorce and with turning fifteen didn't make it any easier. Change-of-address forms make horrible birthday presents.

There were two great things about the move: I was now just two blocks from my guitar buddy Jacob Corry and my mother mercifully ended her short-bus experiment. My sister Beth transferred to a closer school, and my mother begrudgingly accepted that I was old enough to take the subway to Hunter—especially because I could take it with Jacob.

Another positive aspect of tenth grade was that while our

class determined our homeroom, we also had selectives. We were given the choice of physics or chemistry, the choice of art or music, and the choice of gym based on sport; and we were placed in math classes based on how we scored on a test. Most importantly, we were given options when it came to social studies —my worst class.

I was still fighting to keep my grades at a respectable level, so this was a huge relief. At the end of ninth grade, I'd filled out the form to be placed into Ancient Civilizations, since I'd already learned a ton about ancient Egypt in Hebrew school. I figured my prior knowledge would give me a mummified leg up. What I hadn't counted on was that my mother still hated submitting forms on time.

When Jacob and I got to school that first day of tenth grade, we picked up our schedules. Mine said that my social studies selective was Economics, not Ancient Civilizations. This had to have been a mistake. Unfortunately, it was not. The office assistant explained that they didn't receive my form until after the deadline. I still got my first choices of art because music was more popular, chemistry because physics was more popular, and softball because basketball was more popular. But Ancient Civilizations had too many people register, and I was exiled.

I didn't even complain. I just thanked the assistant and moved on. I knew exactly what had happened, and I felt responsible. I should have sat with my mother and watched her sign the form and then walked it to the post office myself. Fool me once, shame on me. Fool me twice, and I am stuck in my second choice of social studies class.

My teacher was a seventy-two-year-old man named Deforest Mikkelsen. This was his forty-eighth year teaching high school, and I liked him immediately. Mr. Mikkelsen was truly funny and taught in a more engaging style than I'd ever seen. He had tons of sayings (my favorite was "Figures don't lie, but liars use figures"), and it became pretty clear that my mother's delay in form-submitting was a huge stroke of luck. Mr. Mikkelsen may have been old, but he was way better than mummies.

On the third day of class, I approached Mr. Mikkelsen on my way out to ask him a question about the homework assignment. As I spoke to him, he was writing numbers next to a few student's names. I didn't know what they meant, but when I saw him write a nine next to my name, I asked why.

"If someone demonstrates a solid knowledge of the material, I give them an eight, nine, or ten," Mr. Mikkelsen responded. "If they show that they clearly didn't do the reading, I'll give them a zero. Everyone else, I leave blank. I factor these numbers in at the end of the year to determine your class participation grades."

I was floored. All I'd done that day was answer a question directly asked of me. It was a basic question, and anyone who'd paid attention at all would have known the answer. And for that I got a nine?

More surprising was that Mr. Mikkelsen's numbers comprised an equitable class-participation grading system. I had had a litany of teachers who factored in class participation based on a feeling at the end of the year rather than your actual work over the course of nine months. A student could do nothing for eight months, have a strong May, and fool a teacher into thinking that they were a better student than they actually were, because they had improved. But *this* system was actually fair.

The next day, I volunteered answers instead of giving them when called on. When I walked by Mr. Mikkelsen's desk after class, I glanced over to see a ten next to my name. My plan was working. I was going to get my grades up just by talking. Actually, Mr. Mikkelsen's plan was working—he'd turned a C student into a B student in one day.

I found myself working harder and studying longer, not just for exams but for classes. I became genuinely interested in the material and had conversations about economics with whoever would participate. I was racking up those tens.

In late October, we were given our big assignment for the semester. We would each write a twenty-five-page paper about an aspect of economics. I'd never written anything that long before, and I was worried about how to do it. But since my paper could be about anything, I chose baseball.

I didn't think I'd get away with that. In grade school, I had to be told that Mets games wouldn't count for current events assignments. In my seventh-grade unit on poetry, I was asked to stop writing so many poems about baseball. And in ninth-grade

English, I was told that W. P. Kinsella's "Shoeless Joe" didn't qualify as classic American literature.

"Sure," Mr. Mikkelsen said when I asked for my topic. "I have no doubt that you'll take it seriously."

And I did. I found every library book I could on the subject and watched all eighteen hours of Ken Burns's *Baseball*. That paper was the first school assignment I finished early (and the first one where I didn't make up an extra book in the bibliography to make it seem like I used more sources). I loved writing that paper. It was the first time I'd enjoyed schoolwork since I'd gotten to Hunter.

On the last day before Thanksgiving break, two weeks before the paper was due, Mr. Mikkelsen wasn't in class. This was not particularly unusual, as teachers got sick, got stuck in traffic, or just took vacation days (as it turns out, some of them were human). Teachers no-showing was common enough that Hunter even had a five-minute rule, where if a teacher (or substitute) didn't show up by five minutes after the class period started, we were allowed to leave. That was probably not a faculty-endorsed rule, but once we all believed it, that rule may as well have been law. If a teacher showed up ten minutes late, there'd be no class to teach and they couldn't really punish all of us. The student who first spread that rumor was a genius.

Something was different this time. When we arrived, Mr. Mikkelsen wasn't there, but a substitute teacher named Mr. Bates was sitting somberly at his desk, not saying a word. Finally, when we were all seated and the class had quieted down, Mr. Bates began to speak.

"As most of you know, Mr. Mikkelsen has been teaching for the last forty-seven years, at Hunter for the last twenty-eight. What you may not know is that he has been battling pancreatic cancer for the last two years. Last night, Mr. Mikkelsen was admitted to the hospital, and it is fairly serious. If you would like to send any cards or flowers, I am sure he would appreciate hearing from his students very much. The address is up on the board."

Nothing Mr. Bates said after that mattered. We did know that Mr. Mikkelsen had cancer, as he'd mentioned it previously. But he mentioned it in a way that none of us took seriously. Mr. Mikkelsen told us that he was given six months to live two years ago so we shouldn't always trust expert opinions. We laughed, as we often did when he spoke, and assumed that this giant of a man couldn't be cut down by something as miniscule as a pancreas. (I think they're miniscule—I wasn't very good at biology.)

After economics ended, I found each of my teachers from my afternoon classes and asked if I could be excused so I could leave early for a Thanksgiving trip with my family. A student leaving early for Thanksgiving was a common occurrence, so none of the teachers had a problem with it. Once I was in the clear, I left school to go to the hospital. I was visiting family, in a way. Family I'd known for only ten weeks—but still, family.

Mr. Mikkelsen was no longer the boisterous big man I remembered. He was frail and quiet and looked like if you folded the hospital bed in half, he'd go with it. When I came in, Mr. Mikkelsen's five decades of teaching took precedence over his health. He said, "Shouldn't you be in school?"

I responded, "Shouldn't you?"

He smiled and told me to sit down, and we talked until daytime visiting hours ended. Mr. Mikkelsen was a baseball fan, and he was curious to see what I'd come up with. I told him about watching Ken Burns and researching the Negro Leagues and how I'd developed a theory that baseball is economically conservative but socially progressive and one how begets the other. As I was ushered out of the room by a nurse, Mr. Mikkelsen told me he looked forward to reading the paper.

I was the first student to visit Mr. Mikkelsen, but I was not the last. As I returned over the next few weeks, the room was always filled with the last five decades of lives that Mr. Mikkelsen had changed. Whatever happened with his pancreas, Mr. Mikkelsen would be living on in a way only the best people do.

I never got another private moment with Mr. Mikkelsen after that first day. And he never read my paper. Mr. Mikkelsen passed away just after the new year.

Hunter held a memorial service for Mr. Mikkelsen, and our class was told that the school wanted one of us to speak about him. I volunteered immediately. I didn't think about how nervous I might be in front of my classmates or what the bullies would say if I messed up. I just knew that if I didn't volunteer, I would regret it.

The auditorium was absolutely packed for the memorial. While I'd spoken publicly in USY, this was bigger than any crowd I'd seen before, and it was a crowd of people who I knew did not respect me. But the importance of what I needed to do outweighed my nerves, and I just started speaking.

The former students that spoke before me painted beautiful tributes of how, no matter how tough Mr. Mikkelsen was as a teacher, he was fair. About how Mr. Mikkelsen's students achieved great things because of how hard he pushed them. About how students learned more than numbers and dates in his classes—they learned *why*.

When it was my turn, I went in a different direction. I wanted to share what I loved about Mr. Mikkelsen. I wanted everyone to remember how funny he was.

So, instead of telling stories of what he meant to me, I just started quoting him.

"There's an equine paradox," I said. "There are more horse's asses than horses."

"In the Soviet Union, everyone is guaranteed the freedom of speech . . . Once."

These were sayings that we all knew, since Mr. Mikkelsen tended to repeat his best material. As the audience laughed, I thought of his smile that first afternoon in the hospital. I smiled, too.

Mr. Bates went from substitute to permanent and graded all our papers. Before he returned them, he announced that there were three A-plusses in the class. Before each one, he spoke about how great the paper was instead of just calling the student's name. Two of them were handed out before Mr. Bates called my name and said a sentence I will never forget.

"Steve Hofstetter," Mr. Bates said. "Let me tell you a little something about Steve Hofstetter."

Mr. Bates went on to say that he'd read my paper multiple times and even shared it with his wife. Mr. Bates said it was the best written paper he'd ever read as a teacher, that it was clear I took the subject seriously, and that he would be surprised if I didn't end up as a professional writer.

I was beaming with pride. In just a few months, I'd transformed from one of the worst students in the class to a student who a teacher was praising in front of everyone. My beam was cut short when Mr. Bates handed me the paper. He'd given me a B-plus.

Mr. Bates felt that, as well-written as the paper was, it could have been more in-depth when it came to my theory that baseball's fiscal conservatism begat its social progressivism. After all of Mr. Bates's bluster about my writing, I had gotten only a B-plus.

That's okay. I'd make sure that my class participation grade would make up for that. Figures don't lie.

BOWLING FOR DATES

I DIDN'T GIVE UP ON GIRLS AFTER THINGS WITH ELAINE hadn't worked out the way I'd planned. I pined after a few others without them knowing. I didn't get any better at attracting women (or even speaking to them), but I was an all-star at hiding my feelings.

I no longer worried about women putting me in the friend zone, because I put myself there before they had a chance to. I could give a tour of the friend zone.

"Hey, welcome to the friend zone. Over there you can see my bed. It's used solely for sleeping."

My vast experience with platonic relationships is what made hitting it off with Hope Womack so surprising.

I met Hope at a USY leadership weekend. The weekend was smaller than a regular Kinnus—just a few people per chapter, so there were only about thirty of us there. The odds I'd meet someone single whom I was attracted to and who was attracted to me were extremely low. As it turns out, those odds were one in thirty.

The odds were almost two in thirty—Hope was there with her identical twin sister, Amy. All the guys knew pretty quickly not to waste our time hitting on Amy. She was a nice girl, and just as cute as Hope (actually, exactly as cute as Hope), but Amy had a boyfriend. Amy didn't just have a boyfriend—Amy had a boyfriend in every conversation.

"I'm sorry my throat is a bit scratchy. I've been fighting a cold," one of us might say. Amy would immediately fire back with, "my boyfriend had a cold once." We learned not to hypothetically ask if he was okay, because that would just lead to Amy saying, "my boyfriend is okay. I have a boyfriend. Have you heard I have a boyfriend?"

I didn't really care that Amy had a boyfriend, since I didn't think she'd be interested in me anyway. I wasn't the kind of guy that girls were interested in. Amy's boyfriend was probably big and muscly and strong, though he may have been weakened by that terrible cold.

I was coincidentally seated near Hope at dinner Friday night, and I made her laugh a few times. When someone asked why Hope had such a unique name, I answered and said, "it's obvious. She was named for the Hope Diamond." When they inquired why one twin was named something unique like Hope and one named something more familiar like Amy, I said, "the Amy Diamond." When you're not trying to impress anyone, it's a lot easier to be funny.

Saturday afternoon, Hope chose the chair next to me for lunch. Well, Hope chose a chair next to Amy, who was already sitting two seats away from me. But Hope could have sat on Amy's other side, and she didn't.

There were empty seats on both sides of Amy, possibly because she was saving them both for her boyfriend. Have you heard that Amy had a boyfriend?

Hope chose to sit next to me, or at least on the side of Amy that was next to me. Maybe her choice of seating had nothing to do with me. Maybe she wanted to be farther from the window or closer to the coleslaw. I was very preoccupied with the seating arrangements of girls I found attractive.

Whatever her motivation, Hope and I sat next to each other and talked through most of lunch. We talked about the differences between Queens and Brooklyn, how you can never be too old to enjoy cartoons, and how we first joined USY because our families forced it on us but now we really enjoyed it. Amy talked about her boyfriend.

By Saturday night, Hope and I had established a rapport. I'd done that with many girls over the years, but this was different. This may not have been platonic. Hope seemed to be as excited to talk to me as I was to talk to her. Was I out of the friend zone? I'd have to update the tour.

"Hey, welcome to the non–friend zone. Over there you can see my bed. It's used solely for sitting on the edge of awkwardly, three feet apart while I obsess over the correct place to keep my hands."

Saturday night's activity was bowling, which played to my strengths. I was not a good bowler, but I was a fiercely self-deprecating bowler. You know who else isn't a good bowler? Most people who are bowling with their youth group. We all sucked, but at least I was going to be funny about it.

The bowling alley was about a mile away, so we all walked. Knowing I needed to find a way to be on Hope's lane at the bowling alley, I asked my friend Abe if he wanted to partner up, and then asked Amy and Hope if they wanted to join us. They agreed, and the four of us spent the whole walk talking. It was perfect—Abe had a girlfriend and Amy had a boyfriend, so they could platonically discuss their love for other people while I bonded with Hope.

Nope.

Abe was more of a friendly acquaintance than a friend, so I didn't know that he and his girlfriend had broken up a few weeks earlier. Amy and her boyfriend were still going strong.

I miscalculated. I did secure a situation where Hope and I would be hanging out all night. But we'd also be hanging out with another single guy who was rebounding and already knew enough about girls to have been in a real relationship.

Amy's boyfriend was also in a real relationship.

On the walk to the bowling alley and throughout the evening, Hope talked to both Abe and I equally. I did everything I could—I bowled terribly and was funny about it just like I'd planned—but there was no shaking Hope's interest in Abe. Abe was a year older than I, which instantly made him a year more attractive. He also had more interesting things to talk about, like heartbreak and loss. I'd had plenty of heartbreak but not much loss. Unless you counted the New York Mets.

By the time we had to head out, I'd given up. I let Abe and Hope talk as I walked a bit ahead of them, trapped in a conversation with Amy about how great her boyfriend was.

"You know who loves to bowl?" Amy asked.

Suddenly, Hope ran to catch up with us and grabbed Amy away from me to speak with her privately. I continued walking alone in a group of thirty people.

After a few minutes passed, Hope came up next to me, and Amy was back behind us talking to Abe. It wasn't until years later that I understood why they'd swapped. While Abe was full-court pressing Hope, I looked like I was confidently walking ahead. Abe reeked of rebound desperation. By giving up, I was back to the version of me that attracted Hope in the first place—the guy who wasn't trying too hard.

Hope and I had a wonderful walk, and we kept talking for the remainder of the weekend. We found an empty room to talk in, hoping to stay until the chaperones caught us and told us to go to sleep. Except the chaperones never caught us. The thing about being a good kid who always obeys the rules is that when you occasionally break one, everyone assumes you have a good reason.

A few hours in to us sharing every story we each had, long after everyone else was asleep, there was a pause. I hadn't even noticed, but Hope and I had been slowly moving closer to one another. By the time we paused, we were arm in arm, with her leaning against me. It was then that Hope kissed me.

I have often wondered how kissing became a fairly universally accepted sign of affection. Before the Internet and TV and talking pictures. Before books and newspapers and maybe even cave paintings. People from all around the world just knew that if you wanted to show someone affection, you opened and closed your mouth on theirs many times in a row like a guppy.

That night showed me how that could have happened. While Hope and I both knew what kissing was, the natural pull to make it happen was something I couldn't explain. Probably because I was too busy making out with Hope to explain anything. When Alexa kissed me, I was excited because I'd never kissed anyone before. But when Hope kissed me, it just made sense. We finally went to sleep around four A.M., regretting that neither of us had packed Chap Stick.

That is how I got my first real girlfriend.

Over the next six weeks, Hope and I made out a lot. We also made our parents drive us to each other's houses. That was particularly important because Hope lived at the far edge of Brooklyn and I was in the middle of Queens. If it weren't for our parents, we'd have only seen each other at USY events.

Sometimes I'd stay over at Hope's house, in a separate room of course. We'd sneak out of our rooms in the middle of the night and make out for a few hours before sneaking back in. I don't know whether her parents knew what we were doing and didn't say anything or whether they were fast asleep because they were tired from all the driving.

When Hope and I couldn't see each other, we tried phone sex. Phone sex was hilariously difficult since we both had big families. Whoever's family isn't home does all the talking, and the other one says "mmmhmmm" in as sexy a way as possible. It was even more difficult because neither one of us had ever done anything more than kiss someone. The rest we were just making up.

Not only had I never had actual sex, but I didn't even have premium cable. My knowledge of sex was based on movies edited for network TV, where you couldn't say dirty words, let alone show what to do with them. I am glad I don't remember exactly what I said to Hope on those calls because I am sure I'd be mortified at my ignorance.

My friends made a lot of jokes about Hope's name (their favorite go-to was asking me if I'd seen her hope chest), but I didn't mind. I had a girlfriend—a real girlfriend—and I was in love. Well, I thought I was.

My logic when I decided to tell Hope I loved her was flawless. I didn't want to break up with her, which meant I wanted to stay with her, which meant I wanted to stay with her forever. And who wants to stay with someone forever if they're not in love? Flawless, huh?

Really, I was just enjoying myself. It felt wonderful to have someone care for me. And when the teasing got bad in school, it didn't matter as much because I had a teammate somewhere. I went to see Hope's plays and got her an awesome birthday present and called her every night.

Dating Hope was much more advanced than dating Alexa and not-dating Lindsay. We were having phone sex and using the word *love* and kissing better than vacuum cleaners. On our sixth-month anniversary (you know, the diamond anniversary), I even got us a hotel room.

Record scratch.

Yes, a hotel room. To this day, it is one of the riskiest, boldest, and dumbest things I have ever done. I took every dollar I had earned from babysitting that I hadn't already spent on presents for Hope and convinced my brother to reserve a room for us at an airport Best Western. We had an elaborate story cooked up—he'd reserve the room since he was nineteen and had a credit card. Then I would show up as his little brother, explaining how his flight was delayed but I was exhausted and if they could just let me in without him that'd be great. My brother went along with it because he also had a girlfriend and lived at home, so he understood my pain. And because I was paying him $20.

Somehow, my story of a delayed flight worked and the clerk checked me in. Probably because the clerk didn't care at all, since he worked at an airport Best Western.

If my brother and I had gotten caught, we'd have been grounded until there was no more ground in the world. And I didn't even really need a hotel room, as Hope and I had only been making out. But it was nice to get some privacy for a few hours. That night, I was making out with my girlfriend in a hotel. This was no longer the friend zone. I wasn't even in the same hemisphere as the friend zone.

An added bonus was that this time, while we were making out, Hope unbuttoned her shirt. I had never seen a woman with her shirt off before, and it would be more than year before it happened again. That alone was worth the risk of being grounded.

The night that I risked my freedom to rent a room in an airport Best Western was a magical night. And it was the last time that Hope and I saw each other.

A week later, we were on one of our nightly phone calls. Hope spent more than an hour telling me the intricate details of a game of tennis she had played while I feigned interest for her benefit. Because feigning interest is what I thought you are supposed to do for someone you think you love.

After Hope had finished with her blow-by-blow recap of her friendly game of tennis, I walked by a newspaper sitting on my kitchen table and noticed a story about a trade the Mets were considering. I commented on it, and Hope *flipped* out.

She yelled at me about how our relationship was one-sided and how I always wanted to talk about me, me, me. I fired back that I'd just listened to an hour of the ins and outs of her tennis game and had made one brief comment about baseball. I spent all day in school keeping to myself; why couldn't I talk about my interests with Hope? She was my girlfriend!

As we fought, I realized Hope was right about one thing: I was always the one forcing my dad to drive me to Brooklyn. I was the one buying her presents. I was the one who risked my freedom to get us a hotel room. The thing she was right about was that our relationship was one-sided, just not the side she believed.

I feigned interest in Hope's tennis game because I always feigned interest in what she was genuinely interested in. I didn't care about tennis and I didn't like going in to Brooklyn and I didn't enjoy watching her plays. I'd rather have talked about Amy's boyfriend.

Hope may have been guilty of ignoring my interests, but I was as guilty of lying about hers. Without realizing it, I had been dishonest with her the entire time. We didn't have much of anything in common—we just really liked making out. We weren't even in love—we just loved the idea of having someone else in our corner. And when I realized the foundation of our relationship was a lie, I ended it. Six months earlier, I couldn't fathom having a girlfriend. And now I was breaking up with one.

I do not regret any of the time I spent listening to Hope talk about tennis or the hours I spent in the car going to Brooklyn to watch her inside joke–filled plays. I learned a lot from that relationship, mainly that you can only pretend to have common ground with someone for so long before you realize that you're actually as far apart as central Queens and south Brooklyn.

The night that I broke up with Hope Womack, I was a very different person than I was the night we first met. I was older. I was wiser. I was more confident. And I had seen a boob.

COACH HOFSTETTER

I WAS LUCKY WHEN IT CAME TO FACULTY IN TENTH grade. Not only did I have Mr. Mikkelsen for economics, but I had Mr. Piccirillo for gym.

Mr. P., as everyone called him, taught a gym elective that consisted of wrestling and softball. Yes, the two great tastes that taste great together. Wrestling and softball was an odd combination, and I wasn't particularly interested in wrestling, but I liked the idea of softball enough to try it. And the alternative basketball selective was paired with track. Running a mile has never appealed to me, so wrestling and softball was my choice.

There's an old joke that goes, "those who can't do, teach. And those who can't teach, teach gym." That was not the case for Mr. P.

Mr. P. taught gym because he loved it. But Mr. P.'s real passion was coaching. Now a Hall of Fame college wrestling coach, Mr. P. still coaches swimming at Hunter. Mr. P. felt about coaching the way I felt about getting to play softball instead of being forced to run a mile.

Gym was always a bright spot for me at Hunter. I wasn't good enough to excel on a team, but put me in a random group of thirty smart kids and I was an above-average athlete. And in gym class, there was no pressure. Gym class wasn't made up of officiated games; gym class was made up of drills. I was good at drills. There was no way to quantifiably lose a drill.

Softball was particularly easy. I didn't have to be taught how to crow-hop or when to throw to the cut-off man. That was stuff I had known from birth. Playing gym softball for me was like the exchange student from Panama taking a Spanish class. They speak Spanish in Panama, right? I never did well in social studies.

One day, Mr. P. told the class he was looking for an assistant coach for the girls' softball team. Student coaches were a regular thing at Hunter. Most teams had a student assistant to help with the equipment, the stats, and other such grunt work. In exchange we got credit toward the seventy-five hours of community service we'd need to graduate. At the time, I associated community service with cleaning trash on a highway, so coaching softball seemed way better. I got the gig.

Before I started, Mr. P. gave me the stat books from the previous year, and I nerdily studied them to see who the best players had been. I was doing that with baseball cards anyway, so why not with people I'd actually meet?

I noticed something odd: There were hardly any stolen bases.

At the first few practices, I stayed quiet and watched. By then, I was good at not making a bad first impression—I'd just not make any impression at all. But eventually, Mr. P. handed one of the practices over to me while he handled some paperwork. I took my moment.

I knew a few of the girls already. Some I got along with, like Sheryl, the president of the improv club. Some I did not, like Alexa Howard, the president of the be-mean-to-Steve club. Alexa had tortured me ever since we'd broken up. She always had a snide comment or rude name for me as we passed in the hallway, and she even purposefully sabotaged a homework assignment when a teacher forced us to pair up. Alexa enjoyed bothering me so much that she found it worthwhile to get a zero. "Zero" was also one of the names she called me in the hallway.

Thankfully, Sheryl was a starter and Alexa was a bench player. So the team was more likely to follow Sheryl's lead.

With Sheryl's help, I got everyone's attention and had the starters go out into the field while I stepped up to the plate. Organized baseball had passed me by, but I could still use my lifetime of baseball knowledge to stay a part of the game. Or a version of the game, anyway.

I took my bat and pointed to centerfield with it like Babe Ruth calling his shot. The girls groaned, rolled their eyes, or made other such gestures that meant "get a load of this idiot." Even Sheryl looked annoyed. But it was all part of the plan. Instead of swinging at the first pitch, I bunted down the third-base line.

The fielders were so surprised by the bunt, no one was in position to field it, and I made it to first easily. They were even more surprised when I didn't slow down, rounded first, and headed for second. Trying to take second is a ridiculous thing to do on a bunt. Which is why they didn't expect it.

The first baseman's hurried throw was wide, and the ball sailed into the outfield as I rounded second, well on my way to third. By the time the left fielder chased down the errant throw, I was already past third and on my way home. The throw beat me home by ten feet, but I ran right into the catcher's glove, knocked the ball loose, and scored.

I'm pretty proud of a lot of my professional accomplishments, but none of them compare to the time I bunted a home run.

"Every time you reach first," I said to the team, "I want to see you on second a few pitches later. If you can surprise them, no catcher in this league has an arm that can throw you out. I want you running. Now, who is up next?"

Alexa continued to roll her eyes, but most of the girls were impressed by the new challenge. As Mr. P. got back over to the practice, he liked what he saw enough to let me run the drills for the rest of the day. By the end, the girls were bunting their way on, taking huge leads, and stealing second. They were high-fiving and cheering for each other and making huge improvements. I could see why Mr. P. loved coaching. Watching such instant progress was awesome.

Over the course of the next few months, I was accepted as a

member of the team. I was a nerdy member whose job included sorting through stats and baking cookies, but I was still part of the team. The girls loved that I posted their stats on the bulletin board, picked a player of the week, and yelled ridiculous things to trick the other teams. A team favorite was waiting till there were two strikes on an opposing rookie. I'd yell to our pitcher, "she's got two strikes, she has to swing!" Our pitcher would fire one out of the strike zone and, more often than not, the bewildered rookie would take a useless hack at it. It only worked once per game, but it worked.

Alexa continued to roll her eyes at me and crack jokes at my expense, but the team liked me and Alexa's barbs were being shouted from the bench, so they were largely ignored. The team was too busy winning to care about what Alexa had to say.

We won. And we ran—oh boy, did we run. The team stole more than four times as many bases as they had the previous year, and we finished 13 and 1 in divisional play. We lost in the playoffs, but it was still an incredible season. I felt great about accomplishing something and even better about accomplishing something as part of a team. I also felt great about girls saying hi to me in the hallway. I had nothing even remotely flirtatious with any of them, but the attention was enough to make me happy.

See that girl who just said hi to me? I'd reassure myself. *She doesn't want to date me, but she respects the hell out of how I keep a scorecard.*

THE SECOND ELECTION

BY THE END OF TENTH GRADE, I WAS GENERALLY FEELING much better about myself. I had friends in USY, the softball team liked me, my grades were going up, and I'd had a girlfriend whom *I'd* broken up with. So I let it ride.

As chapter vice president in my youth group as a sophomore, I was considered an up-and-coming leader in the organization by all the staff. To have the staff like you is not the key to popularity. But some of the students liked me, too.

There was, however, a divide between the popular kids and the ones who were considered up-and-coming leaders by the staff. When girls talked about who they thought was cute, they never complimented anyone on their leadership skills. I know because they had the discussion of who they thought was cute right in front of me. Usually about my friend Mason.

Carter Sokol was another one of the boys everyone thought was cute. Carter had flowing blonde hair and was muscular and thought it was hilarious to moon people. Meanwhile, I parted my red hair, was scrawny, and changed in the bathroom so no one would see my underwear. Carter and I were extremely different. And we ran against each other for vice president of the division.

The division was one step up from the chapter, and it encompassed all of New York City. Winning uncontested in my chapter was one thing, but the division was a different animal. And since I didn't have good hair or big muscles or a lack of shame, my only chance at beating Carter was to be funnier than him. He could charm the crowd all he wanted, but if I was funnier, I could potentially win everyone over. I worked on my speech for weeks. If there was one thing I knew about kids like Carter Sokol, it's that they weren't likely to put the work in.

The plan was to have Mason nominate me with a funny speech. I took the girls' conversations I'd been overhearing about cute boys and translated them into utter buffoonery.

The crowd was read a page from my nominator's "secret diary" where, instead of discussing my qualifications, Mason talked about how dreamy I was. Everyone there knew I was qualified, but what some of them didn't know was that I was fun, too. Mason finished, and I took the mic. I paused, shuffled my papers, cleared my throat, and flexed my scrawny right arm like I was on Muscle Beach.

The crowd laughed, and from then on I had them. That nomination speech was the opposite direction from where everyone thought I'd go. Instead of showing that I was an up-and-coming leader, I showed I was human. When the staff called my name as the winner after the votes were tallied, the room applauded.

I had to wait until the school year started again in order to actually be the vice president. Over the summer, I was bored, I was broke, and, now that I was single again, I was lonely. *Single again*—that was not a phrase that came naturally to me. For so long, *again* was not part of that phrase. I was just single as if it were a perpetual state of being. It was Newton's Law—a red-headed nerd uncoupled stays uncoupled. And as someone who wrote jokes paraphrasing Newton, staying uncoupled seemed like it was going to happen for me.

I learned that some kids from USY were working at Ramah, a summer camp in upstate New York. And one of their families was asking around to find an extra babysitter.

Babysitting made me money, but it did not make me cool. Women in their twenties and thirties are attracted to men that are good with kids, but that instinct doesn't kick in until after high school. My classmates got their money from working in fast-food places or from playing poker or (in The Clique's case) from simply having parents. I got mine from changing diapers.

But babysitting was something I could do for the summer. I could make some money, tell bedtime stories to practice my improv, and perhaps work on my newfound ability to make friends.

I took the job, and I went upstate. I'd spent my life in New

York City and had never spent more than a few nights away from home before. But I committed to work for ten weeks at a summer camp, living in a staff bunk with a bunch of strangers.

The quiet and shy kid I'd developed into was officially dead outside of Hunter. He was replaced by someone with confidence who sought out attention and who had even had a real girlfriend once. I tried not to bring that up too much, lest Amy pop up over my shoulder to remind me that she had a boyfriend.

I packed all the hand-me-downs I owned into a hand-me-down duffel bag and headed to a tiny town named Wingdale. But the day before I left for Ramah, I did one more crazy thing—I got an extremely stupid haircut.

I was not the first fifteen-year-old to get an extremely stupid haircut, and I am sure I was not the last. I wasn't rebelling or trying to make a statement. I was, however, trying to be cool. The problem with trying to be cool is that when you put effort into being cool, you're inherently uncool. But at least I no longer parted my hair, because the entire left side below where the part had been was now just red stubble. I had shaved one-third of my head.

This was not a popular haircut or one I'd ever seen before. I was just sitting in the barber's chair wanting to shake things up. If you're having trouble picturing it, imagine someone with a side part. Now, shave everything beneath the part clear off. And then please stop laughing.

People who didn't know me may have thought I was punk

rock, until they noticed I was wearing a baseball T-shirt with Looney Tunes characters. The good thing was that no one in the staff bunk was cool. Anyone spending their summer working as a babysitter at a Jewish summer camp is inherently uncool. So, in relation to everyone else, I was somewhere in the middle.

Whether or not we were cool in the general sense of the word, a hierarchy does form in every group. My haircut prevented me from being at the top of this hierarchy. But I risked being solidly at the bottom when I unpacked and made my bed.

The only bed sheets I had brought, because they were the only bed sheets I had, were the Smurf sheets I'd slept in since I was two years old. My parents had not yet caught up with their children getting older. And since my parents were the same people who spent weeks fighting over ratty towels, buying me new sheets because I was going to camp wasn't going to happen. I didn't have to take the Smurf sheets to camp—I could have borrowed Beth's Bambi sheets, Strawberry Shortcake sheets, or other Bambi sheets. Smurf sheets were the obvious choice.

As I'd finished making my bed, one of my bunkmates (who I could already tell was going to fill the cool vacuum in this hierarchy) asked, "why the hell do you have Smurf sheets?"

I responded, "the chicks dig 'em."

The rest of my bunkmates laughed. I wasn't serious—other than Hope, no woman I wasn't related to had ever seen my Smurf sheets. Hope had never commented on them. I just said it because I thought it was funny.

There is a valuable lesson that I was just starting to learn: People by nature are self-conscious, so if you project confidence, they will retreat. The reason my "chicks dig 'em" joke worked is because the bunk bully was expecting me to retreat. Not caring what people say about you is a tremendous weapon against bullies.

The would-be bully's power was removed entirely an hour later when three of the female staff members came to the bunk to introduce themselves. Pleasantries were exchanged and we all made plans to sit together at dinner, without knowing that there was a staff table we were all supposed to sit at anyway. As the girls left, the cutest one of the three pointed to my bed and said, "I like those Smurf sheets!"

She said it genuinely, so she was not expecting the big laugh her compliment received. I thanked her and she left, a bit more confused than she had been when she walked in. The bunk hierarchy had been established, and I was at least toward the top of the middle.

As the summer went on, the babysitters spent most of the days together watching our kids play as we got to know each other. We talked about everything from high school to our families to the results of the *Cosmo* magazine quizzes that the girls always wanted the guys to take. There is something incredible about a bunch of teenagers who have never had sex taking quizzes to determine whether or not they were selfish lovers.

At night, we told jokes that were inappropriate to tell around the kids we took care of. A lifetime of listening to stand-up and years of being quiet in my high school hallways meant I knew thousands of these jokes. I regaled my new friends with bar jokes, light-bulb jokes, and (for those with a darker sense of humor) dead-baby jokes. The only thing worse than virgins taking quizzes to see what kind of lovers they are is a group of babysitters falling out of their chairs laughing over dead-baby jokes.

I was enjoying holding court with my new friends, but as the summer moved forward, they began coupling off. Some would declare themselves boyfriend and girlfriend one night and be broken up the next, while others were together the entire summer. The proximity that camp provided made it hard not to be attracted to each other. I am guessing that's how Alexa Howard found her camp boyfriend.

I'd had a crush on the girl who complimented my Smurf sheets since the first night. Perhaps it was because she had inadvertently bailed me out of what could have been a tough situation. Or maybe it was because she was cute and often flirted with me. Either way, her name was Charlotte, and I thought she was the best.

One night, I asked Charlotte to take a walk with me. Everyone in camp knew what that meant, but I still had to go through the formalities. I may as well have said, "would you like to be alone with me so I could tell you that I like you and maybe we could make out a bit?"

Charlotte said no.

What? Who says no to an innocent walk? How did she know I was going to tell her I liked her and hope she'd make out with me? You know, aside from everyone knowing that's exactly what "would you like to take a walk" meant.

Charlotte's *no* surprised me, because I'd gotten a great vibe from her ever since that first day in the bunk. She always listened to my stories, and she laughed at my jokes. So why didn't she like me?

Since there were only two dozen of us and we spent fifteen hours a day with one another, I was able to find out through gossip pretty quickly. Charlotte didn't like me because I liked myself too much.

Charlotte complained that I was always monopolizing conversations and that I was always telling stories about myself, which are also two descriptions of stand-up comedy. At first, I brushed off Charlotte's rejection as ridiculous. How could anyone monopolize conversation? If you want to say something, say it. And who else am I supposed to tell stories about, if not myself? Am I supposed to regale people with stories from someone else's perspective?

Charlotte, unfortunately, was right. I was so happy with my new ability to be interesting that I forgot how to be interested. While monopolizing conversations and telling stories about yourself can make you a great stand-up comic, it also makes you pretty annoying to talk to.

I was confused. Here I was, finally comfortable enough to talk to someone who wasn't my girlfriend, and she was rejecting me because I was talking too much. I was running my mouth because I had years of silence to make up for. I'd tell Charlotte all about it, but I'd have to tell the story from someone else's perspective for her to enjoy it. Man, she is going to hate this book.

Charlotte complaining I had an ego was a setback, sure, but a necessary one. After years of being shy and quiet, the pendulum had swung too far in the other direction. I had gotten drunk with attention and, frankly, didn't know how to handle it. Charlotte's rejection, in the long run, would be a positive thing. But at the time, I had to learn how to cope.

THE PRANK WAR

THE PRANK WAR STARTED NATURALLY. I HAD THREE close friends at camp—Ari Landau, Eyal Dar, and Nate Boxer. Ari was younger than the rest of us and sensitive about it. We didn't care, but there was obviously a part of him that felt less than because he didn't have the life experience we had. Though most of our extra life experiences involved getting turned down by girls.

Every day, the four of us met at a picnic table after breakfast to hang and talk while making sure the kids didn't do anything dangerous. Or dangerous enough to get us fired.

One day, Ari arrived clearly upset. Charlotte had said something that really bothered him, but he wouldn't tell us what. Nate asked if she'd turned him down for a walk, and we all laughed. It's amazing how much intent factors into how hurtful people can be. I had no problem with Nate teasing me about my rejection, because I knew he meant well.

But if our bunk cool guy had made fun of me, I would have been livid.

And that's what happened to Ari. He told us that Charlotte had called him a little boy. And not in an aren't-you-cute way. She knew he was sensitive about his age and she said it anyway, intending to hurt him. He'd stormed out of the room silently.

Eyal suggested that we do something to get back at her. As the ball-buster of the group, Nate had no problem with that. And it was hard for me to turn down something that could get a laugh. It would be a great way to show Ari that he was a respected part of the group. And it would be more fun than just sitting at a picnic table.

The mistake people often make when planning a revenge prank is going overboard. I believe the hallmark of a good revenge prank is letting the punishment fit the crime. Charlotte had purposely said something hurtful, so the best way to get her back was to make her feel guilty about what she'd done.

The four of us came up with a plan. We concocted a story that Ari was actually three years older than the rest of us but suffered from a rare disease that made him look younger. I pulled Charlotte aside that night to explain to her how what she said had really hurt Ari.

I enjoyed the charade, probably more than I should have. I liked defending my friend. I also liked practicing improv.

Charlotte fell for our ploy and asked me all the questions we had predicted and prepared for. What's the disease called (poliponesia), how long has he had it (his whole life), who else knows (just Nate and Eyal), and so on. We saw those questions coming. And then, there was one question we hadn't thought of.

"If he's older, wouldn't he be in college now?"

"It comes with a learning disability," I explained, leaning on my improv experience. "That's why he was so upset when you called him a little boy. That's why he stormed out."

Charlotte followed the pattern we assumed she would. Even though I swore her to secrecy, she approached Nate and Eyal to ask them if it was true. As planned, they pretended to be upset with me for telling her and said I needed to stop talking so much. That was something we knew Charlotte would agree with.

Later that night, Charlotte approached Ari and told him how sorry she was, how she never should have said what she'd said, and how she hoped he could forgive her. Ari said he hoped that she could forgive him for making it all up but was glad to know she was sorry. This time, Charlotte was the one who stormed away silently.

Anyone who has ever been involved in a prank war knows that was not where things ended. Charlotte spent the next two weeks stewing over how she was going to get back at me and Ari. She didn't seem to think Eyal and Nate were in on the prank; Charlotte assumed that we had tricked them, too. Maybe she didn't want to admit that she was the only one gullible enough to believe such a ridiculous story. But when she finally had her plan, she asked Eyal and Nate for help. That is like asking the Secret Service to help you kill the president.

Charlotte's plan was completely uncreative—to sneak into our bunk while we were sleeping and pour water in our beds to make it look like we'd wet them. To get away with it, Charlotte asked Nate and Eyal to tell her when we normally went to sleep. This was ridiculous for a few reasons. Aside from telling our close friends what she planned on doing to us, hers was an impossible question to answer. We didn't have a set bedtime. And if she did want to know whether we were asleep, she could have just snuck over at four A.M. and knocked on the door gently (to be safe) and seen whether anyone was up.

Nate told her we went to bed around eleven on Thursdays because we worked early Friday mornings, a preposterous answer since we were rarely back at the bunk before one A.M. The answer was even more preposterous because she was usually out that late, too. Sometimes people believe what it is convenient for them to believe.

It was extremely difficult to feign sleep that night. We were giddy, knowing what was coming. We held to my *the response to an action must match the original action* prank philosophy and rigged a water bucket and trip wire on the inside of the door. And to make it more fun, we all went to "sleep" with water balloons under our blankets. If she wanted to wet our beds, we'd wet her.

When Charlotte came in, she brought a few of the other girls with her. Thankfully Charlotte entered first and caught the brunt of the bucket. We sprung out of bed fully dressed and started throwing the balloons, and the girls stormed out of the bunk—not silently at all.

Ari, Nate, Eyal, and I tossed some towels down on the floor and headed to the staff rec room to play some ping-pong. It was only eleven-thirty—way before our bedtime.

That is how most of the summer went. The girls were constantly trying to get revenge for something that Charlotte had started in the first place, and we were constantly foiling their plans. At Hunter I had Jacob and in USY I had Mason, but in a few short weeks at camp I now had a group of friends that had my back completely and were there for me in times of war. Even if it was only a prank war.

Pretty quickly, the girls weren't upset anymore. Instead, they were having fun trying to pull one over on us. Once, they put a few dozen Dixie cups in our beds while we were out. So we covered every inch of their floor with them. Once, they put an open, upside-down bottle of water on our bunk porch so that if we picked it up, it would spill everywhere. So we did the same thing to every porch in camp except theirs (including our own), thinking everyone would blame them.

I loved every minute of the prank war. I even loved the minor pranks the girls got away with, as those pranks gave me reason to come up with the next bit of justice. I loved the creativity involved. And years of being bullied made me very interested in people getting what they deserved, even if it was all in good fun.

One night, the prank war finally ended. There was a staff

building with a porch that the girls would often sit out on, and you could get to the porch roof from the second floor windows. I loved sitting out on that roof at night. From up there, you could see above some of the trees and watch the moonlight hit the lake. We were just ten feet above everyone else, but it felt completely private. It probably would have been a great place to take a girl, if the one I'd liked earlier in the summer didn't hate hearing me speak.

The guys hung out up there pretty regularly, and one of the girls always thought it was dangerous. She freaked out constantly about how we were going to slip and fall and end up in a mangled heap. We grew tired of her incessant lecturing and decided that for our next prank, we would end those lectures.

We took a dummy left over from a camp play and we dressed it like me. That wasn't too hard—we just had to find the right ugly hand-me-downs. Then we gave it my jacket and my hat with an orange rag underneath it.

With the girls on the porch below, I loudly wondered how close to the edge I could get without falling. I then did an old magician's trick—I programmed the girls to truly believe I was up there and close to the edge by poking my head over the side of the roof. The guys held my legs, just in case. I was mischievous— I wasn't insane.

When I knew the girls saw me hanging over the roof, I disappeared back up as Nate loudly warned me to stay away from the edge. I laughed and said I was indestructible. And then we hurled that dummy over our heads like an out-of-bounds soccer ball. Maybe it was more like a mini-basketball, because that's what doubled as the dummy's head. Which was perfect, since the head bounced just a bit before settling in a mangled heap.

Nate ran downstairs and burst out the door and yelled, "Oh my God, is Steve okay?!" I followed close behind Nate and yelled, "Oh my God, am I okay?!" The horrified-yet-angry looks on the girls' faces were well worth the many slaps on the shoulder we received soon afterward. I was surrounded by friends. Not just Ari, Nate, and Eyal, but the girls, too. That prank war made us all into allies.

Throwing fat, dead me off a roof was the last shot fired in the prank war. Maybe it was because that was the last week of camp, or maybe it was because it's hard to top faking your own death. Either way, we won. Which was particularly gratifying since it all started when someone criticized one of us for being immature.

THE PLAY
IS THE THING

JUNIOR YEAR WAS WHEN I STARTED FEELING COMFORT-
able at Hunter. I had found a few of friends, the softball team
was on their way to another first-place finish, and my grades
were floating well above C-level.

Mr. Mikkelsen had definitely affected my approach to school
(and to life). Another reason I was able to pick my grades up is
that I became increasingly able to pick my classes.

We went from selectives (where we had a choice between
two or three types of the same class) to electives (where we
could choose any class we wanted). The first class I chose was
creative writing.

Creative writing was wonderful. It was taught by a funny
(and often stoned) middle-aged woman named Mrs. Acker. Our
assignments were to write poetry, plays, short stories, and other
things I'd been writing during my lunch breaks anyway. Humor

was rewarded in Mrs. Acker's class and I coasted through with As on almost every assignment.

I have always loved storytelling. I grew up creating silly stories with my sister, and now I got to write and be rewarded for it. It almost seemed unfair in the best way possible.

Another reason I loved Mrs. Acker's class is because, like a youth group, a creative writing class is self-selective. Bullies don't know how to express themselves creatively—that is why they are bullies. My creative writing class was filled with people like me—it was the Freak Hallway, but in chairs.

One of those creative people was Katie Averill. Katie was a senior, but she took the time to say hello to me after class, by name. Katie didn't just smile in my general direction, or even kind of look at me like other girls I'd made the mistake of thinking might like me. Katie actually said, "Hi, Steve!" and asked about my weekend and complimented my work.

Katie's writing was fantastic. When she read to the class, her stories made me laugh, her poems made me sad, and her smile made me melt. I didn't have the guts to ask a senior out. But man, I loved going to that class.

As much as I loved creative writing, the thing I still enjoyed most was improv.

We weren't breaking any comedy ground: Most of our meetings consisted of re-hashed games from "Whose Line Is It Anyway." Okay, all of our meetings consisted of rehashed games from "Whose Line Is It Anyway," except the ones where we'd watch bootlegged copies of "Whose Line Is It Anyway." But I loved every minute of it.

That the improv club met on Mondays was fortuitous—the meetings gave me a reason not to dread the end of the weekend, and some happiness to start off the week.

One Monday, we had something different to discuss: auditions for Brick Prison.

Brick Prison, named for Hunter's castle-like exterior, was our student-theater company. Hunter was a very arts-friendly school, and not just because of the Freak Hallway. We had three big plays every year: a classic like *Death of a Salesman* or *Arsenic and Old Lace*, a musical like *Jesus Christ Superstar* or *Grease*, and the homegrown Brick Prison.

Brick, as it was affectionately known, was the most revered. Brick was made up of five student-written, one-act plays. Unlike the classics and the musicals, Brick was student-run from start to finish.

When I was in elementary school, I had the lead in all the school plays. I wasn't a good actor; I was just one of the few kids who could remember his lines.

Hunter was different. There was so much talent at Hunter. I had already tried out for Brick the year before, and I was cast as a nonspeaking extra, sitting at a bus stop. At least I had no need to go to rehearsal—I had plenty of experience waiting for a bus.

Junior year, I had a lot more confidence—both in myself and in my improv abilities—so I tried again. And this time I did it a little differently.

The audition consisted of reading a monologue. The majority of students who were auditioning read one of the provided selections. I asked if I could read something I'd prepared instead. When they said yes, I launched into the "Who do you love? You love a car!" monologue from *Ferris Bueller's Day Off*. It worked—I was cast as the comic relief in one of the plays.

My role was small but fun. In a dream sequence of an otherwise serious play, I was one of two over-the-top TV announcers commenting on one of the characters climbing a building, risking their life to save another's. My scene closed with me excitedly proclaiming, "They both could die—let's watch!"

I loved getting laughs, and unlike in improv club, there would actually be an audience this time. Also, the star of one of the other acts was extremely talented, and it was wonderful to learn from him even though he was only a sophomore. And my hilariously over-the-top co-anchor was a girl named Amalia who was best friends with Katie Averill.

Amalia and I had a great time hamming it up in our roles as the most insensitive news anchors in history. And during the final show on Saturday, we decided to push it further.

The final performance was always prank night, and pranks were something I'd gotten pretty good at. The idea was that the crew would mess with the actors in ways that wouldn't be obvious to the audience, and the actors would have to power through as if nothing was wrong. A coat rack might be on the wrong side of the stage. There might be pornography inserted into the book an actor was reading. Or, like when I was a sophomore, they might send in one of the nonspeaking extras dressed in a trench coat, pretending to flash the rest of the extras at the bus stop while the stars couldn't see what was happening behind them. I enjoyed wearing that trench coat.

Amalia and I decided to add a gag to our script, where the announcers kept getting each other's names wrong. At first it'd be hard to notice, but eventually, she was calling me Barbara and I was calling her Stanley. Our ad-lib got a tremendous response from the crowd and made us wish we'd have used it during every show and not just prank night. I understood then why Hope had loved her plays so much.

My other moments in the sun came in between acts. As the crew rushed around changing the set, some of the cast from the various plays acted out short sketches, and I got to be in two of them. One was improv, showcasing one of the same "Whose Line Is It Anyway" games I'd done a hundred times. It was an incredibly short set change, so I was only able to get one joke off. But it worked, and I felt great.

The other sketch I was in was a bit longer. The talented sophomore I was learning from wrote a *Saved by the Bell* parody that I happily participated in. I believe that *Saved by the Bell* is simultaneously one of the worst and best shows in television history, because it was such cheesy garbage, but it was so much damn fun. The sketch crushed (harder than Amalia and my name gag) and it felt good to be a part of it. Everyone cheered, especially for the sophomore who wrote it. I said it then and I will say it now: Lin-Manuel Miranda is extremely talented.

By the end of that final night, I got to be in three scenes, and all three killed. The thing I didn't learn about comedy until years later is that it doesn't always work when you need it to. Sometimes you put yourself out there and fall flat on your metaphorical face. But not that night. That night, it was perfect.

I was pretty emboldened. Not emboldened enough to ask a senior like Katie Averill out, but emboldened nevertheless.

THE THIRD ELECTION

I WAS VERY PROUD OF THE WORK I'D DONE AS THE DIVI-
sional vice president of USY. I did the social stuff, like organizing a few Kinnuses. I did the administrative stuff, like
organizing the meetings. And I did the community service
stuff, like organizing letter writing campaigns. USY was called
an organization, after all. I figured I should be organized.

It was rare for a junior to be vice president, and kind of perfect since that meant I could easily run for president. And, just
in case there was any doubt as to whether or not I could handle
the increased responsibilities if I won, the president got sick.

No, I was not involved in anything nefarious. Two
months before elections, the president was hospitalized
with what he later learned was Crohn's Disease. The doctor said to eliminate all stress, so he stepped down and asked
me to take over. I agreed and became acting president of the
division.

As the election approached, it looked like I would run uncontested for president. Why shouldn't I? I was already president. I was already vice president. Hell, I did two jobs for the price of one.

More important than that, people genuinely liked me. Well, some people did. Some people did not like me. Rachel Farb was one of those people.

Rachel Farb was a bully from a family of bullies. I don't know what happened in that house to make the Farb kids such jerks, but it was working extremely well.

Rachel's older brother, Doug, was my brother's best friend. Doug was a little guy for his age (which still made him a big guy for my age), and he thought he was hilarious. Doug wasn't funny at all—he was just mean. Yes, sometimes mean jokes are funny. Sometimes mean jokes are really funny. But Doug was the type of guy who would shove someone into a wall and think it was the cleverest piece of comedy ever created. That someone he shoved was usually me.

David would discourage Doug from his barrage of sticks, stones, and names, but he never stopped him. Perhaps David was afraid of Doug, too.

I don't throw around the word *hate* without careful consideration, but I hated Doug. Whenever Doug came over to hang with David, I tried to not be there or I'd find a way to not be seen. That got a lot harder when we moved four people into a two-bedroom apartment in Forest Hills. In the hundreds of times I saw him, Doug never said a nice word to me. I don't mean he never paid me a compliment—he never even said *hello* without following it with an insult. Doug is now a special education teacher—a particularly ironic profession considering how often he gleefully called me retarded.

Doug once came into the room I shared with David, asking if I'd seen his sneakers. I said no as quietly and politely as I could, lest I disturb his thousand-year slumber. He began looking around my room and asked if I could help him. So I did. I got up and began looking around with him. It was the only time Doug and I did anything together without him mocking me or punching me. That didn't last.

When I got near the closet, Doug shoved me from behind. I went head first into the wall and fell in a heap of Steve. As I clutched my bloody nose, Doug laughed hysterically.

"I know where my sneakers are! I can't believe you fell for that, you retard!"

That was Doug Farb. The guy that makes fun of you for trying to do him a favor.

But the most *Doug* story I can tell is how he became David's best man. David got married that year, which thrilled me. Not only is a wedding typically a happy and joyous occasion, but it meant David was moving out. I would get my own room, and David's wedding would be the last time I ever had to see Doug Farb.

I did not expect to be David's best man, though I certainly would have enjoyed it. Someone's best man is an extremely personal choice, and David had to choose between his brother and his best friend. Even at the time, I got that David was in a difficult spot and that the choice was not easy for him. Objectively, it made more sense for David to choose me. Friends come and go, and David and I weren't inseparable, but we were certainly close enough. David and Doug drifted apart after David got married, and I'd be surprised if David has seen Doug even once in the last decade. But I get that David couldn't have known that would happen ahead of time. Even if I did.

When David sat me down to tell me that he'd chosen Doug, he explained that he knew I'd be okay with the choice, but that if he'd chosen me, Doug would have been angry.

"I *am* okay with the choice," I said. "Though you knowing that Doug wouldn't be okay with it is exactly why you shouldn't have chosen him."

Rachel Farb was just as bad as her brother. She never physically harmed me or threatened me, but she was as big a thorn in my side. Perhaps even bigger, because I had to work with her.

Rachel was also on the divisional board of USY, as director of membership. She skipped half of our meetings, and she constantly mocked me and interrupted me at the ones she did attend. Also, she was horrible at her job—she didn't run a single event targeted at driving up membership numbers. Under Rachel, the division's membership declined for the first time in more than a decade. Perhaps we lost members because no one wanted to hang out with Rachel Farb.

The most underhanded thing that Rachel did was not skip all her own work but take credit for mine. There was an event we'd been holding in the same location since before my siblings were in USY, so I suggested a change to keep it from going stale. That was one of the few meetings Rachel actually attended, and she fought me on the idea. Not the way Doug fought me, but she fought me.

My idea prevailed, the change worked, and the event was a huge success. So Rachel stood in front of the group and took credit for the whole thing. My ego was bruised, but at least I didn't end up with a bloody nose.

When Rachel announced that she was running against me for president, that was the first time either Farb made me laugh. But since Rachel was serious, I decided to take it seriously, too.

A third and fourth student jumped into the fray also, but those two were freshmen who hadn't even held a position in their chapter before and were running as goofs. I didn't pay them much attention. I figured, if anything, they and Rachel would split the wholly unqualified vote, making my election even easier. And if I didn't have enough of an advantage, that year the elections were held at my home chapter, ensuring that I'd have maximum friend turnout.

I wrote a speech about my qualifications—how I'd already been president and how I knew what it took to do the job. I talked about how I'd organized events and how I'd organized meetings and how I'd organized letter-writing campaigns. And as I sat down, I smiled, because I knew I had it wrapped up.

My smile faded quickly. Rachel started her speech by saying, "I could tell you stories about what I've done in my position, but I don't have stories. I got plans, baby."

I wanted to yell that she couldn't tell stories about what she'd done in her position because they'd all start and end with her skipping meetings and taking credit for other people's ideas. But I couldn't. It'd be pretty rude, but more so, I already knew I was in trouble. Rachel was giving her version of the classic "I promise soda machines in the cafeteria" speech. Her plans were nonsensical, poorly thought out, and impossible to execute. But no one cared.

Rachel did the only thing a wholly unqualified candidate could— she brushed her lack of experience under the rug and lied to everyone. And, like it has a million other times in history, it worked.

The election was set up so that if no candidate had a majority, there'd be a run-off between the top two. With four people running, I assumed that a run-off would happen. I was wrong again—Rachel won on the first ballot. I didn't just lose—I got completely spanked. The division didn't want to vote for someone who was organized. They wanted to vote for someone who had plans, baby.

After the vote, I was asked if I intended to run for any other positions, as that was the option of anyone who was running for president. I declined. And I walked to the back of the room in stunned silence.

Mason came over, grabbed me by the arm, and walked me out of the room. "You don't need to torture yourself," he said. "It's over. There's nothing you can do now."

For the next twenty minutes, Mason and I just walked around the block. At first, I blamed Rachel's inane populist speech and the other students for letting it work. But as Mason and I talked it out, I realized that my original assessment was wrong. They didn't care whether I was organized or not. They cared about me being their friend. I lost because I didn't have as many friends as I thought I did. And Mason helped me realize that was okay.

I had spent so long being ignored in school, that when I found USY, I wanted everyone to like me immediately. I had forgotten— or perhaps I'd never known—that friendships are forged over more than just seeing people once every few weeks. Mason wasn't just a USY friend; he was a real-life friend. We'd hang out outside of USY, we knew each other's families, and we talked about who we dated. Actually, we talked about who Mason was dating and who I wanted to date. The point is, we were friends.

And no one else in that room was my friend. I thought they were, because I could hold their attention, they were happy to see me, and sometimes I could make them laugh. The lessons I should have learned from Hope and Charlotte were coming together. Making people laugh didn't make them my friends. That made them my audience.

I didn't lose because of Rachel's empty Coke-machine promises or because the members bought into them. I lost because I was so busy worrying about what people thought about me that I hadn't taken the time to ever think about them. It wasn't enough to get people to like me. I also had to afford them the same courtesy.

I walked back into the room and watched the rest of the election unfold. The results were fairly predictable, just as the race for president was if I had truly thought about it. As each winner was announced, I smiled and applauded, and I meant it. And when it was all over, I walked up to Rachel.

"I wanted to congratulate you," I said, to her confused silence. "I'm glad you won."

I didn't say that to confuse her, although it was fun to know that it had. I said it because I meant it. I wasn't glad she won because I thought she'd make a good president; she was just as unqualified as she had been an hour earlier. I was glad because a burden was lifted off of me. Instead of spending the next year trying to impress everyone, I could spend it forging actual friendships like the one I had with Mason.

I walked back over to where Mason was standing and found him talking to a few other people.

"You guys want to get something to eat?" I asked. They did, and we all went to grab some food. Maybe I would become friends with some of the people in that group and maybe I wouldn't. But I was, at the very least, going to try. And, hey, I could certainly organize a group to go get some food. Organizing was what I was best at.

BLAZERS
AND ZOMBIES

WITH THE STRESS OF THE ELECTION (AND HOLDING ANY
position of responsibility in USY) gone, I focused on my creative writing and improv. I also focused on people. I had spent so much time feeling persecuted and sorry for myself that I hadn't learned how to really make friends. I had some, but they were all people who made more of an effort than I did, and I realized that not everyone would extend themselves like that. To actually get to know people, I had to be the one reaching out.

I started in the least likely place. I started with Katie Averill.

Since Katie had already been saying hi to me before class, I started saying hi to her after class. And then I started sitting next to her, and working with her during group projects, and actually getting to really know her as a person.

I knew from Amalia that Katie thought I was funny—Katie had loved our little name stunt during prank night. So one day, I gave Amalia a call. "I heard you're going to junior prom," I said, since I had heard Amalia was going to junior prom. It made sense that she'd be there. Amalia was a senior, but her boyfriend was a junior.

Amalia and I talked about how she was strangely excited about it even though she'd been last year and she had her own prom coming up a few months later. Amalia was excited because this time she felt like she got to be a guest at someone else's party. The only problem was that none of her senior friends were going.

"Maybe one is," I said. "I'm going to ask Katie."

Amalia practically burst through the phone. I was sure that part of Amalia's excitement was having a friend that might be going to the party with her. But she also went on and on about how she had always thought that Katie and I would make such a cute couple and it was a wonderful idea and she was rooting for me and several other encouraging statements. Amalia also said that I'd better ask Katie soon, since it was going to be hard to keep that a secret.

I called Katie right after I hung up. I didn't have the guts to get rejected in person, but Amalia's excitement had excited me.

Katie and I talked about the latest assignment, a modern satire of a great work. I was planning on writing a version of "The Raven" about high school, an idea that Katie seemed to like. After all, she was writing a high-school version of *Macbeth*. We were in sync in many ways. And then, I just said it.

"Do you want to go to the junior prom with me?"

Katie said yes immediately. There was no time to blabber about how I thought it made sense for her to go because Amalia was going or to add in an *as friends*. Katie had said yes.

I didn't know what to expect from junior prom when I got there. The last school dance I'd been to was the first school dance I was able to go to. I was so excited for that one—Hunter had a few dances each year, and when the first dance came around, I put on my best ugly shirt (I wasn't fashion forward enough to know that orange shirts are a bad idea for a redhead) and stood there awkwardly while everyone ignored me. From then on, school dances weren't my thing.

I had spent the previous three years at USY dances though, so I wasn't intimidated by junior prom. I just wanted to know what I was in for. Jacob Corry's girlfriend was a senior, so she became my Obi-Wan.

Jacob's girlfriend explained that junior prom was less a prom and more a fancy dance. There were no limos or corsages or tuxedos. The guys who owned suits would be wearing them, but half the students would probably be in a blazer and khakis. And it wasn't like prom where dates showed up together. The long-term couples did, sure, but most of the dates just met each other there.

Armed with the knowledge of what to expect, I met Katie there. Sort of. I showed up, and she showed up, but it became pretty clear that we weren't really there together.

What happened between Katie's immediate yes and her arrival to turn us so utterly platonic? Did Katie not understand

I had asked her as a date? I specifically didn't say *as friends*—she had to have known the difference. She was a worldly senior, after all.

Then it hit me. Katie was a senior, and she couldn't go to junior prom unless a junior asked her. And she wanted to go to junior prom with her best friend. It didn't matter that Amalia thought Katie and I made a cute couple. Katie didn't agree, and her opinion on the matter was way more influential.

I gave my theory one final test. A slow song came on, and I approached Katie from across the room. Because that's where she was hanging out—completely across the room.

"Let's dance," I said, with the courage of a man who had nothing to lose. Not "Would you like to dance?" or "I was just thinking, maybe we should dance?" But a confident, assured, "Let's dance." That was the kind of thing that a boyfriend would say to a girlfriend if she was his date at the junior prom. So why couldn't I say it to my date?

Katie took my hand and we walked to the dance floor, and we danced. If you could call what we did dancing. We stood as far apart as we could while still technically touching and took small steps from side to side. My hands did their best to be on Katie's hips, but her hands were not on my shoulders—her finger tips were on my shoulders. Had a casting director been there, Katie would have been given the lead in any zombie movie she wanted. What we did was as much dancing as sleeping is strenuous exercise.

After our non-dance, it was pretty obvious that Katie had just used me as an entry point to the party. So I did what anyone should have done in that situation. I danced by myself.

I didn't intend to dance by myself. The sting of my zombie realization was too fresh for me to do anything fun. But dancing was my only choice.

There are very few situations where someone has no choice but to dance. Maybe someone is shooting at their feet in an old western, yelling "dance, monkey, dance!" Perhaps they're in a coming-of-age movie where dance is the only way for those young whippersnappers to express themselves. Or, in my case, they are shoved into the middle of a circle and have to choose between fight or flight.

I'd been to enough USY events to understand that most high school dances consist of circles of half a dozen to a dozen students dancing not too close to each other. Sometimes, the circle becomes an opportunity for a student to show off, or for a couple to try to demonstrate just how in love they are by grinding their pelvises against each other's knees. Or the circle can become one more place for Scarlet Daly to try to embarrass you.

What Scarlet didn't realize when she pushed me into the middle of that circle was that I was not the same meek kid who had tried to defend myself by quoting *Gone with the Wind*. I had spent the last three years in USY as part of dance circles—just not in front of anyone who went to Hunter.

So as the music played, I danced. Whether I was an objectively good dancer or not didn't matter. I was so much better than everyone expected me to be, I may as well have been Beyoncé. You know what? Still a strange sentence to write.

I danced and I danced and I danced. And as the crowd started chanting "Go Steve!", two senior girls I didn't know jumped in the circle to dance with me. I went from humiliation and regret to dancing with two other people's dates in the length of one song.

As the song finished, everyone cheered, and the two seniors hugged me. Well, not everyone cheered. I saw Scarlet fuming. I caught her eye, smiled, mouthed *thank you*, and started dancing to the next song.

Rejection is an odd thing—it only matters if you give it the power to matter. If you've ever called into a radio contest or played the lottery, you know that rejection without consequences exists. Why don't we get upset when we're not the ninety-ninth caller? Why don't we cry when we scratch off a ticket to find it doesn't have our numbers? Because we've already accepted those things as possibilities before we extended ourselves. And relationships are no different.

"Most people," my brother had said years earlier, pointing at the middle of three lines, "live their life here. They don't go far down, but they don't go far up either. The further you go toward this top line, the further you will also go toward this bottom line. You decide if that's worth it. I've never been a fan of the middle."

Ever since then, I'd been taking more and more risks. I'd been stepping further toward both the top and bottom lines. And, overall, I'd been happier. I resigned myself to never live my life in the middle again. Unless it was the middle of a circle of people chanting "Go Steve!"

At the end of the night, I was exhausted from all the dancing and was about to grab some food and take the long subway ride home. Jacob and his girlfriend invited me to come with them to eat.

"You sure?" I asked. "I don't want to push in on your date." They laughed; they'd been dating for a while at that point and to them this was just a regular Saturday night, only with more formal attire. "Besides," Jacob said, "You think Katie is eating alone? I bet she's with Amalia right now, being consoled about how she missed her chance to dance with you."

I laughed at the nonsensical thought of Katie even caring about us dancing together, and the three of us went to one of those little all-night delis with upstairs seating somewhere in midtown. Jacob teased me about how naïve I was to expect a senior to date me, as his senior girlfriend playfully punched him in the arm. After we ate, we walked around Manhattan for hours, just talking and laughing about how everything had unfolded.

It wasn't until that night that I learned the full lesson from my heart-to-heart with Mason. I didn't need to work on making more friends, and I certainly didn't need to work on any more dates. I needed to spend time with the friends I already had.

HEAD

LINER

ROCK, ROCK, ROCKAWAY BEACH

I WASN'T OFTEN INVITED TO PARTIES. MOST OF THE TIME I didn't even know they were happening.

It made sense that parties existed. Every high school movie I saw had wild parties. I never thought much about why we didn't have any at Hunter. I assumed that there were no parties because we were in the middle of a big city and students were scattered throughout it. As it turned out, the reason I didn't think there were any parties at Hunter is because I was not invited to them.

Backstage during Brick, I overheard two girls talking about who had hooked up at the party the week before. There was a rumor that one of the girls had gotten an STD and her parents found out, and now they were going to prevent her from going away to college. And all I took away from that story was, "there was a party?"

It's like that old proverb: "If a party happens in the forest, and no one invites you, does it make a sound? And is that sound you watching Twilight Zone reruns at home by yourself, weeping softly?"

I did have a social life outside of high school. Not just my USY social life—I'd go out with my classmates sometimes. I'd get Chinese food with Rebecca Chaikin or play basketball with Ozzie Roberts or shoot pool with Jacob Corry. I really enjoyed playing pool. I'd have grown up playing if my parents' pool table hadn't been leaning up against a wall in the basement next to the filing cabinets.

Sometimes a bunch of us would all go to Brent's apartment to play video games because his parents were never home. Never. They may or may not have existed.

But parties were not a thing I did—not since the debacle at Marley's country house. At the end of junior year, one of the Freak Hallway students I was friendly with had a party I was actually invited to. I asked my mother if I could go, and her usual strictness was replaced by enough confusion such that by the time she figured out what she was saying yes to, she'd already given me permission.

Actually, my mother didn't really know what she was saying yes to. All she said yes to is "can I stay over at Noel's house on Friday?" When she asked who Noel was, I had a fit about how my mother never paid attention to anything I said and how was I supposed to make any friends if she didn't even pay attention to the ones I had. I told her that Noel lived in Queens, just like us, and that if she was uncomfortable, I would be close by. Amazingly enough, that all worked. And suddenly I was going to a party.

Noel lived in Rockaway, which is technically a part of Queens in the way that Guam is technically a part of the United States. Actually, it might be easier to get to Guam than it is to get to Rockaway.

There's a Ramones song about Rockaway, and the chorus says, "It's not hard, not far to reach. You can hitch a ride to Rockaway Beach." The Ramones are liars.

Breezy Point, the part of Rockaway where Noel inconveniently lived, was a forty-minute drive from my apartment and virtually impossible to get to by public transportation. If you try to get directions to Breezy Point today, Google Maps will tell you, "Sorry, your search appears to be outside our current coverage area for transit." That's how you know a place is hard to get to—when Google has to apologize.

Had Google Maps existed then, the directions probably would have been, "Take a right out of your apartment, and give up completely. Have you considered not going to this party?"

I had not considered that. This was my first real high school party, so I wasn't going to let distance prevent me from going. Noel was a theater kid like I kind of was, so I wasn't worried about the bullies being there. Also, bullies don't take two trains, a bus, and a cab to go to parties.

A few of us hung out at Hunter after school that day and went to Rockaway together. That kind of insane public transportation isn't a problem when you're being an idiot with your friends. I felt bad for the commuters on the trains and bus we took. Not just because we were being loud and annoying, but because they had to commute to and from Rockaway every day.

By the time we arrived, the party had already been going for an hour. Some of the seniors in attendance got there much quicker because they drove—cheaters.

Despite my initial excitement, there wasn't much for me at a party. I didn't drink or smoke (which might have been why I was not invited to other parties). And I wasn't particularly good at striking up conversations with strangers. I spent the first hour there talking to the friends I had come with. Which was fun enough, but it wasn't two-trains-a-bus-and-a-cab fun.

A blonde girl I didn't know joined our conversation. I wasn't paying much attention. Having been so burned by the Katie situation, I wasn't looking to meet anyone new just yet. And that is how it always works. The best way to succeed at attracting someone is to not care whether or not they're attracted to you. Eventually, the conversation became just Colleen and me.

Colleen Barrett was a senior at Hunter, and she was a theater kid, too, but she was involved in musical theater, which is why I didn't know her. Also, she was on the crew side of things, so I wouldn't have even seen her in a play, had I ever attended any of the plays I wasn't in. Colleen and I were completely new to each other, so we had an awful lot to talk about.

Colleen and I talked until the sun came up. Literally, until the sun came up. Those still at the party (which was most of us—there's no good way out of Rockaway at one A.M.) walked down to the beach and watched the sun rise over the Atlantic Ocean. It was the kind of moment that makes two people who have been talking all night kiss for the first time. And that is how I got my first adult girlfriend.

After the sunrise, we all went to a diner and got breakfast, before starting our long journeys home. New York City has a lot of wonderful facets to it, but one that is not complimented enough is the availability of all-night diners. Especially ones that can accommodate a few dozen very tired and somewhat hungover teenagers. Colleen and I sat next to each other. Astonishingly enough, we still had more to talk about.

I got home two and a half hours after I had left the diner—Rockaway is hard enough to commute from, but it's even tougher on a Saturday morning. I didn't mind. I slept for most of the ride, making sure to not fall too deeply asleep lest I miss my stop. I'd honed the skill of not sleeping through my subway stop during my commutes to high school, and it might be why I'm still a light sleeper today. If my brother, David, had had that skill, I'd still have my original Nintendo.

I mainly didn't mind the commute because I was happy. It had been more than a year since Hope and I had broken up, and the connection we'd had over six months didn't even compare to the connection Colleen and I made in one night. Colleen was intellectual and worldly and had experienced things in life that I'd only read about. And she'd read about everything. Colleen had opinions on authors I'd never even heard of. I'd never heard of the people on Hope's tennis team either, but I was much more interested in the authors.

When I got home, my mother told me I had a message from "a girl named Colleen." Ever since that mystery girl called me about the physics homework, I'd made sure my mother took down messages more carefully.

I called Colleen back immediately, and we talked more. How could two people have this much to say to each other? Colleen had been bullied a lot earlier in school and had also gotten quiet. She'd found theater crew as a way out of her shell, and now she was just making up for lost time. She was a lot like me.

Eventually, Colleen had to hang up because her mother wanted the phone. But before she did, Colleen asked me a question that surprised me.

"So," she said, making her question more casual than it was, "What are we?"

I was so surprised, I didn't even know what she meant. We'd made out, didn't that mean we were boyfriend and girlfriend? I was so naïve, I was unaware there were other possibilities.

A more experienced person would have known that we could be seeing each other, just talking, friends with benefits, or a host of other euphemisms for not exclusive. But I learned about dating from romantic comedies. And only the kind of romantic comedies my parents would let me watch. So I didn't know *not exclusive* was an option.

"As far as I know," I said naively, "you are my girlfriend."

Colleen took my answer to be sweet and confident, and she agreed. I didn't learn until months later that she was not expecting me to say that.

After that, Colleen and I spent as much time as we could together. Colleen lived on the Upper West Side of Manhattan, which made things difficult. But the Upper West Side is much easier to get to than Rockaway, so I didn't mind.

What made things more difficult was that Colleen's mother hated me. I was taken aback—while girls rarely liked me, their mothers always thought I was great. It makes sense: I was smart, polite, and not likely to assault their daughter. I wasn't even likely to make out with their daughter.

Colleen told me to not take her mother's abrasiveness personally, as her mother was like that with everyone—especially men. About a month after we started dating, Colleen confessed that her father had been murdered when she was a little girl, and her mother was never the same after that. Whoa. This was heavy stuff. I didn't know if I was ready for an adult relationship.

Colleen also told me something else that surprised me. The reason she started talking to me that night was because her friend Julia had a crush on me and she was doing reconnaissance. I'd never met Julia, but she used to refer to me as "the cute boy in my creative writing class," and Colleen was about to leave the party when I walked in. When Colleen saw me, she stayed to get some details and report back to Julia. After Colleen and I had been talking for a few hours, she excused herself to use the restroom. Really, she was calling Julia to check if it was okay to date me.

Learning about Julia made me wonder if anyone else had ever had a secret crush on me over the years. I'd had secret crushes on plenty of other people. Perhaps someone had one on me. That is a thought you should hold on to—there are billions of secret crushes out there in the world. Someone you've never met might have one on you.

I knew my relationship with Colleen likely had a shelf life. I was already committed to working at Ramah for the second half of the summer, and Colleen was going off to college before I'd get back. But we used what time we had together. I went to Colleen's apartment twice before her mother made that not very fun, but she came to mine as often as possible. I even picked Colleen up from her part-time summer job. Okay, so I met her after work and we took the subway together. But in New York City, that counts as picking up.

I was almost seventeen and Colleen was already eighteen. Colleen was a very sexual person, and we fooled around as often as possible. Because it was the summer and school wasn't in the way, "as often as possible" meant almost every day. It was all pretty exciting stuff; Colleen taught me more about anatomy than I'd ever learned in school. Like I said, I never did well in biology class.

When it was time to go back to Ramah, Colleen and I broke up. We'd only been together about six weeks, but it was a great six weeks. I learned a lot from her—including that life can be a lot more complicated and much darker than school bullies. And, while I was at Ramah, I made sure to read a few of the books Colleen had recommended.

I'd spent so much time feeling sorry for myself that I never realized how much harder other students had it. Here she was—bullied as much as I was, but also the daughter of a murdered father and a suspicious, frightened mother. I was upset that Tommy Tillet pulled a chair out from under me. The whole world had pulled a chair out from under Colleen.

I classify my relationship with Colleen as my first adult relationship because at the end of it I felt like much more of an adult, and Colleen must have felt like an adult for a very long time. And, almost as important as that, I got to go to a party.

WHEN I FOUGHT A RAPPER

AS MUCH AS THEO WEBSTER TERRORIZED ME, I WAS
never truly afraid for my safety until I met Phillip Cuchillo. I
was afraid Theo would hurt me, sure, and I was afraid of what
that pain might feel like. But I knew deep down that if Theo did
anything to me, it would be temporary. And the older we got,
the less I feared Theo actually doing anything. There are only
so many years someone can threaten you before you figure out
they're all talk.

Phillip was different. Theo was a good student who liked
to feel powerful. Phillip was an aspiring criminal. There were
rumors that he brought weapons to school and rumors that he'd
killed people and other rumors I didn't believe. Hunter was a
difficult academic school that you had to pass optional tests to
get into. Menaces don't take optional tests.

Friends of mine from USY went to city schools and had to
deal with actual deliquents. Some of my friends from grade

school even became actual delinquents. But I didn't believe what they said about Phillip. You don't rob a liquor store and then study for your AP art history test.

If you're a fan of hip-hop, you may know Phillip by his stage name. One of his ablums even hit number twelve on the hip-hop charts. This was before all that.

During a free period, I was sitting in a fairly empty hallway struggling with writer's block when Phillip ran by, laughing. Right behind him came Rory Daniels, the girl I'd had an unrequited crush on at the very beginning of high school. She was laughing, too.

"Come on Phillip!" Rory said. "Give it back."

Phillip stood at the entrance to the stairwell, tauntingly waving Rory's jacket at her. That's when Rory asked me to help.

She seemed to be having fun with whatever was going on, so I figured it was some sort of game of keep away.

Sure, I thought. *I'll play.*

I had writer's block anyway, and here was a cute girl asking me for help. Phillip seemed to find the whole thing funny, too— maybe this would be a way for me to ingratiate myself to this "hooligan" everyone seemed so scared of.

Phillip bolted up the stairs, and I gave chase. He wasn't running particularly quickly, so I was able to catch up with him by the time we reached the fourth floor. I didn't know what I intended to do when I caught him. Maybe I'd ask him how long he'd had a crush on Rory and laugh with him about how I once did, too. Maybe I'd thank him for letting me play along. Maybe I'd make sure he didn't stab me with the enormous knife he pulled out. Yeah, that last one. That seemed most important.

When we got to the fourth floor landing, Phillip turned and pulled out the biggest switchblade I'd even seen in person, partially because it was the only switchblade I'd ever seen in person. Even if I had seen others, Phillip's blade still would have been bigger. There's an iconic scene in Crocodile Dundee where a mugger demands Dundee's wallet after pulling a knife. Dundee says, "That's not a knife. *That's* a knife," pulling out an enormous bowie knife. Phillip's switchblade was somewhere in between the two.

"Go back downstairs," Phillip said with an icy stare. I have no idea if Rory got her jacket back that day. I just know that I went downstairs.

After that, Theo Webster didn't seem like such a big deal anymore. I did what I could to avoid Phillip, although he didn't seem to be concerned with me. I am guessing I was not the only one he had pulled that knife on. And with the pressures of AP tests and the demanding schedule of crime, he couldn't be troubled to keep track of every single student whose life he'd threatened. Not without some sort of criminal administrative assistant.

A few weeks later, I was out in Hunter's courtyard after school ended. It was common for a few of us to play basketball for an hour or so after classes, so the day seemed pretty normal. That changed quickly.

One of my teammates was my friend Ozzie Roberts, a fiercely intelligent and extremely athletic black student I'd met back in my Mirta short bus days. On the other team was a kid named Elba, a somewhat intelligent and somewhat athletic black student. After Ozzie spin-faked Elba and drove in for an easy layup, Elba threw the ball at Ozzie and called him an Oreo.

For the uninitiated, *Oreo* is a pretty demeaning thing to call a black person. It means black on the outside, white on the inside and is code for telling someone that they're not black enough. As someone who grew up with a black sister in a white family, I had heard the word often, and it bothered me. But it bothered Ozzie more, because he knew why Elba was saying it.

It was not the first time Elba had called Ozzie an Oreo. Elba took exception to Ozzie's choice of extracurricular activities, as Ozzie was the star of the school's debate team. It was Ozzie receiving an award for debating that led Elba to first call Ozzie an Oreo. And, on this particular day on this particular basketball court, Ozzie had had enough.

Ozzie caught the ball with one hand and beaned Elba with it.

Ozzie wasn't upset that he was being called white or that he was being called not black enough. He was upset that Elba, as a fellow black student, believed that academic success somehow made you white. Ozzie was proud of his accomplishments, as he should have been. And he didn't want someone like Elba making him, or any other black student, feel less than for those accomplishments.

This was not my fight, but Ozzie was my teammate and friend, and I agreed with him. So I had his back (as much as someone unwilling to fight could have someone's back). I'd been in one fight at Hunter before, when I was sucker punched in the stomach for not giving up control of a handball court. That was the day that I learned that getting punched isn't nearly as bad as the fear of getting punched. Though not getting punched will always be way better than both of those options.

As far as Elba knew, I was willing to fight for Ozzie, and so was the rest of my team. So before a real fight could break out, Elba needed to take stock of exactly what he was getting himself into.

It was then that I saw Phillip coming toward me. Phillip hadn't been playing or even near us when we were playing. But Phillip loved a fight, so when he saw one brewing, he ran over and did the creepiest thing I've ever seen anyone do. Phillip, with a razor blade in his mouth, walked right at me and said (in the muffled way people speak when they have razor blades in their mouth), "Come here, Steve. Give me a kiss."

Yes, Phillip had a razor blade between his teeth, pointing outward. Phillip wasn't just an aspiring criminal—he was a super-villain. Suddenly I believed all the stories. Maybe Phillip *had* robbed a liquor store. Maybe Phillip *had* killed someone. Phillip definitely brought weapons to school.

In that moment, I thought of trying to trip Phillip. If he was dumb enough to put a razor blade in his mouth, he could swallow it, for all I cared. The reason I didn't is best said by another iconic movie scene, this time from *The Usual Suspects*: "How do you shoot the devil in the back? What if you miss?"

Instead of tripping Phillip, I backed away.

"This isn't my fight," I said to Phillip, clearly cowering. "I'm just playing basketball."

Phillip took the blade out of his mouth and laughed at my fear. Fear is what he got off on.

Unlike the first incident, this one had witnesses, and word got around about it quickly. I didn't tell any teachers or administrators, because expelling someone isn't the same as arresting them. Let's say someone wants to stab you and you get them expelled. That doesn't protect you; that provides the stabber more free time to stab you. I let the rumors swirl without confirming anything, and eventually it was chalked up as just another Phillip story.

As time passed, I got back to the grind of school and tried to forget about the razor blade incident, or at least as much as you can forget about someone threatening to cut your tongue out. Other people remembered it, too.

Later that year, a sophomore named Sasha brought a knife to school, too. He didn't intend to use it; he just wanted to scare someone. Sasha found out that his girlfriend had cheated on him with his friend Jared, and he wanted revenge. And when Sasha confronted Jared in the hallway and pulled out that knife, it was obvious Sasha immediately knew he'd made a mistake. When

Jared started walking toward him, Sasha threw down the knife and collapsed, crying. Sasha had never intended to hurt anyone, and he also didn't actually hurt anyone. The poor kid had let emotion get the best of him, and an otherwise sweet kid did something extremely dumb.

Unfortunately for Sasha, everybody saw his fight. And more unfortunately, that everybody included a teacher, who reported it immediately. No adults had witnessed either time Phillip had pulled a blade on me, so he faced no repercussions. But Sasha was suspended immediately.

This was a big deal—yes, Sasha did something extremely reckless and dangerous. But it was clear to anyone who knew anything about the situation that his intent wasn't to cause any harm. Sasha just wanted answers for why he was in so much pain. And now he was being punished for it—the type of punishment that could potentially cost him his choice of college. This suspension could have a ripple effect that would severely damage Sasha's future. Meanwhile, Phillip got to walk around with a blade in his mouth like it was no big deal.

The injustice of that juxtaposition became the subject of several student inquiries as to why Sasha had to be suspended. Sasha's classmates were rallying behind him—something I fully supported. The only problem was that in order to make their point, those students repeatedly told Hunter's administration that Phillip had not been suspended for pulling a knife on me. Once the administration had been told that by enough people, they acted.

When I say they acted, I do not mean they did anything to protect me, or even to attempt to protect me. I was called into the principal's office, with Phillip, and was told to tell the story of when Phillip pulled a knife on me. How could the administration possibly think that was a good idea? Sasha was not the only dumb one at Hunter.

I said, "no, thank you." I'd rather have been sucker punched in the stomach.

Dr. Haanraats, in the genius way that only he could, threatened to suspend me if I didn't start talking. Somehow, I was in the wrong for having an instinct of self-preservation. I was caught between a rock and a sharp place.

Extremely reluctantly (and with Phillip sitting in the chair next to mine), I told Dr. Haanraats about the time Phillip tried to kiss me with a razor blade in his mouth and ended the story with, "Can I go now?" Dr. Haanraats demanded to know about the other time. Dumbfounded, I asked him what he meant. "In the stairwell," Dr. Haanraats said. "There wasn't a time in the stairwell?"

"Oh," I said. "I think Phillip was just playing around then. I didn't even remember that till you mentioned it just now."

Like hell I didn't remember it. I didn't understand why I was being forced to talk about it or how anyone else knew about that incident. And I didn't understand why, if the school knew about both incidents, they hadn't done anything to protect me before now. Or *during* now.

"I hear this shark tried to eat you twice," they may as well have said. "So we've decided to cover you in fish blood and sit you next to him. Now, taunt that shark or you'll be suspended."

The worst part was that Dr. Haanraats had no intention of exonerating Sasha. He just wanted to use the information he was getting to discipline Phillip as well. Sasha's punishment was upheld.

And in the most insane turn of events, Sasha was suspended and Phillip wasn't. The rumor was that Phillip's father was a lawyer and threatened to sue the school if any action was taken against his son. Even if that was just another Phillip story, the school had the information they needed to do something about Phillip, and they did nothing. There was absolutely no reason to put me in harm's way like that. Dr. Haanraats was a principal, yes. Principled? No.

I don't know if Phillip respected that I obviously tried not to snitch, or whether he was too busy assaulting other students to assault me. Whatever the reason, Phillip thankfully didn't seek retribution, and I never heard from him again.

Unless you count his music.

KING HOFSTETTER

HOMECOMING IS A PRETTY BIG DEAL FOR A LOT OF HIGH school students. But at Hunter, homecoming isn't a deal at all. We have our traditions. Every spring, Carnival turns our schoolyard into a county fair, with booths and games and funnel cake. For two weeks in May, Killer turns our seniors and juniors into teams of assassins, shooting each other with toy guns for cash and bragging rights. And we used to have a fall trip to Bear Mountain State Park each year, until a ninth-grader snuck alcohol in and ended that tradition pretty quickly.

Homecoming is a football-based tradition, and there isn't really any high school football in Manhattan. There certainly wasn't at Hunter—even our baseball and softball teams played their games in the city-owned fields of Central Park (and only when permits and schedules allowed).

I can't say for sure whether Hunter had a Homecoming Dance

every year or my senior year was the only time we experienced it. It could have been a tradition we usually ignored. Or homecoming could have been a one-time gimmick, a renaming of the fall dance, to get people to think it was more important than it was.

By senior year, I hadn't just found a few friends but a group of them. I was still friends with Jacob Corry and Rebecca Chaikin, but there was also Randy Grier-Holmes. Randy was a fellow card and pool player and one of the only people on the baseball team I truly liked. Randy was also childhood friends with my friend Mason from USY, which bonded us more. And I'd become closer with Ozzie Roberts. Perhaps something good came out of Mirta's bus after all—fear really does bring people together.

There were lots of other people Randy and Ozzie were friends with, and I started hanging out with them, too. There was Roy Benton, the whip-smart political science junkie who was perpetually frustrated with his long-term, Mormon girlfriend, Cathy. And Nick Giannopoulos, the not-so-smart but sweet oaf who wasn't very frustrated at all with his equally not-so-smart girlfriend. There was also Dan K. and Dan C. and Joe J., who was only called Joe J. because we enjoyed the alliteration. And of course there was Brent, whose parents were still never, ever home.

I was only close with Jacob, Randy, and Ozzie, and casual friends with the rest, mainly because I didn't know how to hang out after school. I spent so much time at Hunter not having friends that now that I'd finally made them, I didn't know how to initiate spending time around them. I just quietly waited to be invited to hang out with people.

From seeing me dance at junior prom and his friendship with Mason, Randy knew that dancing was something I enjoyed doing. When Randy asked whether I was going to go home between school and the homecoming dance or go straight there, I didn't know what he was talking about.

"There's a homecoming dance?" I asked. "Did we suddenly get a football team?"

When I saw that Randy was serious, I deflected as if I had known about the dance all along and asked what his plans were. He said he was just going to kill time between school and the dance as it wasn't worth it to take the subway all the way home and back just to be home for an hour.

"Yeah, me too." I said, fishing for more information. "It's next week, right?"

Randy laughed. "It's today, bright child. You really didn't know about it?"

Homecoming wasn't the first time that I had been out of Hunter's social loop, so I accepted my ignorance and came clean. There are two groups of people who don't know about school dances. Those too cool to be bothered with such things and those not cool enough to be bothered with such things. I was clearly in the latter camp.

Randy told me that there was no dress code and that what I was wearing would be fine. Which was good, because even if I had gone home, I didn't have a nicer baseball T-shirt or a better pair of non–purposely faded jeans I could have changed into.

I spent the next few hours hanging on Hunter's steps with the group, as we talked about which girls we thought were cute and teased Roy that maybe he and Cathy would hold hands for the first time. Well, I watched the other guys do all that stuff—I was quiet, just happy to be included. I'd grown bold in USY, but I was still pretty quiet at Hunter.

At six P.M. the dance started, but it wasn't time to go to the dance. We had to wait until six-thirty. If you've never been to a school dance, you should know that you never, ever get there when it starts. You never want to be the first one there, standing by the drink table in a mostly empty gym, trying to not look like the loser who is by himself at the drink table in a mostly empty gym. I say this as someone who spent the first half hour of his first dance by himself at the drink table in a mostly empty gym.

Instead we went for pizza and strolled in at six-thirty like we had planned. That is what the phrase *fashionably late* means. Fashionably late does not mean you should be so late that you miss your Little League game.

The dance was uneventful but fun. I mainly outer-circle danced. I wasn't about to grind with anyone I would see in class the next day, and one middle-of-the-circle dance at junior prom was enough for me. I didn't need to replicate that at homecoming.

At the end of the dance, our class president (Cathy) got on

the mic and told us it was the moment that we had all been waiting for. As someone who hadn't even known the dance was happening until lunchtime that day, I was not really waiting for any moment. Still, I applauded along to fit in.

"It's time to announce the homecoming court!" she said with a level of excitement matched by no one else in the room. Even Roy couldn't pretend to be interested, and he was still trying to get Cathy to make out with him.

In other schools, homecoming court is as big a deal as the homecoming game. But since we still didn't have a football team, this was probably just another gimmick to make the dance interesting.

There hadn't been any elections, further convincing me that homecoming was a made-up thing. Allegedly, the names had just been pulled out of a hat. I began doubting this was true, as it was far-fetched that the organizers knew who was at the dance, let alone that they would go to the trouble of putting all their names in a hat. And if they were drawing out of a hat, wouldn't they do that in front of us? Also, whose hat? I had so many questions.

Great, I thought. *Something else rigged in favor of the popular kids.*

When Cathy announced Roy as the court jester, everyone got a big kick out of it, and it further cemented my theory that there was no hat involved. I was all but certain that this thing was fixed when the homecoming princess and prince were one of Cathy's friends and one of the Dans. But I started enjoying the fix.

Sure, it was fixed, but it was fixed in the right direction for once. So much of high school orbited around the popular kids. They seemed to get everything they wanted, and here was a time where they finally didn't. Even though this was a made-up honor at a made-up dance that they probably didn't want, it was nice to see the good guys win.

When Cathy called out the name of our homecoming queen, my theory vanished like it was Brent's parents. The name she called out was a name I would have expected her to call out when I thought the system was rigged in favor of the popular kids. The name she called out was The Clique's most revered member: Victoria Layton.

I haven't yet mentioned Victoria because we may have been in the same high school, but we were never in the same strato-sphere. There is a girl at every high school who is perfect, and ours was Victoria Layton. She was beautiful and rich and a straight-A student and funny and kind. I never heard anyone every say a bad word about Victoria Layton, and in high school people say bad words about everybody. Victoria was like Scarlet Daly, if Scarlet wasn't cartoonishly evil.

After the Stephanie Spencer incident, I steered as far clear of The Clique as I could, but I got to know Victoria senior year. Our math teacher assigned our seats and happened to assign mine next to Victoria's. She didn't pick our names out of a hat either— Hofstetter and Layton had five students between them, and there were five students per column. Our math teacher preferred to go alphabetically front to back, which left Victoria and me as row buddies. That's just basic math.

It took a while for me to be comfortable sitting next to Victoria. Even before she was announced as homecoming queen, she was royalty. At first I was afraid Victoria was just like everyone else in The Clique, but I quickly learned she wasn't. Victoria struck up conversation with me every day, asking me about the homework and about life in general. I knew she wasn't interested in me romantically, and that's not just lack of self-confidence talking. Victoria had been dating Eugene Kwok, a fellow Clique member, since they were in elementary school together. Unlike Roy and Cathy, Victoria and Eugene had likely been holding hands for quite some time.

And so, Victoria and I were friends. Not hang-out-after-school friends or phone friends or even lunch-as-friends friends. But we were math-class friends, and I genuinely looked forward to catching up with her in the five minutes before class started each day. Victoria was way too studious to talk during class.

The fix made more sense now. The inconsequential positions were given to Cathy's friends, but homecoming king and queen still went to The Clique. If homecoming was rigged for the popular kids like everything else was, at least Victoria was the one to get a victory. I was happy for her. Sure, Victoria won at everything else, too. But I'd rather Victoria get a victory than Scarlet.

As the prerecorded drum roll for homecoming king began, I

stood back and waited for Cathy to call Eugene's name. Only, Cathy called my name instead.

I have never had a moment of bigger disbelief in my life than when I heard the words *Steve Hofstetter* said into that microphone. If homecoming was fixed, why the hell would it be fixed for me? I was barely a peripheral part of the group of friends it was fixed for. And even though Victoria was not, she and Cathy always seemed to get along. Maybe Victoria winning was Cathy's effort to make it look like homecoming court wasn't fixed. Maybe I was overthinking it.

I didn't get to say anything to Victoria that night, as being crowned—verbally—was the last thing that happened at the dance before everyone went home. But on Monday in math class, I brought it up first thing.

"Congratulations on homecoming queen," I said.

"Thank you, my liege," Victoria responded, bowing. "How ridiculous was that?"

"Yeah," I said. "Homecoming king was never something on my to-do list. Especially since we don't have a football team. Maybe I'll put it on my college applications as if it was real. That whole thing was a bit of a farce."

"I know!" Victoria responded. "We didn't even get a coronation dance!"

At that moment, our teacher told us to open our textbooks. And that was the last Victoria and I spoke of homecoming.

PROFESSOR
HOFSTETTER

I HAVE ALWAYS LOVED TEACHING. AS THE YOUNGEST KID
in my family, I enjoy having a chance for people to look up to
me. Even more so, I like feeling needed. I'd guess that if you
polled one hundred teachers, you'd find a solid number of
youngest children and people who grew up needing to be
needed.

Most of my "teaching" experience came from babysitting. I
also volunteered to run the kids' classes for my synagogue, but
that consisted mainly of reading to children who were too young
to sit still in the service. The classes were run by teenagers who
didn't want to sit still in the service.

Senior year, I was given the chance to teach for real. Hunter
had an option where seniors could, instead of attending one of
our own classes, teach someone else's. I jumped at the chance.
Not only could I get my teaching fix, but I could get out of a
class, too. As someone who grew up trading baseball cards, I

knew a good deal when I saw one. Teaching a class instead of attending a class was like being given a Ken Griffey Jr. rookie card instead of attending a class.

We weren't full teachers, obviously, and we didn't get paid. We were interns for existing instructors. Most teaching interns were tasked with the ever-important job of grading pop quizzes and collecting homework. I had had teaching interns throughout high school and never given much thought as to how a student became one or why. I didn't like most of my interns, as teachers had a tendency to make their interns play bad cop. Being the one to grade pop quizzes and demand homework rarely ingratiates you to a classroom.

My situation was a bit different than that of the other interns because I actually got the chance to teach.

I was interning for Mrs. Acker, my oft-high creative writing teacher from junior year. If you've ever had a teacher that you felt was genuinely rooting for you at every step of the way, you have had your version of Mrs. Acker. She smiled often, encouraged everyone, and allowed her students to succeed by eliminating their fear of failure. She was a joy to be around. Also, she sometimes got high and forgot to come to class. So I taught.

The class I interned for wasn't creative writing; it was a freshman English class. My responsibilities started out small. Mrs. Acker would let me lead one specific class here and there. Eventually, she had me coming up with my own assignments. And by November, I was teaching one full day a week.

Mrs. Acker didn't just encourage creativity in her students, but in me, too. Standing in front of a room of thirty students wasn't much of a departure from the improv club or my speeches in USY or the softball team. I was timid at first, but I got increasingly bolder as the year went on. Eventually, I gave myself permission to improvise.

In most non-math Hunter classrooms, the chairs were set up in a U formation around the perimeter of the room. When we administered exams, the chairs were put in rows so the students couldn't cheat as easily. It was a system many teachers used, and a system students were very familiar with. One day, the students arrived to find the chairs in rows and started complaining about getting a pop quiz. I told the students there was no quiz—the chairs were just set up that way because there had been an exam during the previous class period. None of the students believed me.

The students kept assuming there must be a quiz. Some asked me how much it counted toward their grade, some made excuses as to why they couldn't finish the reading in time, and one accused me of being an out-of-touch aristocrat (we were reading Julius Caesar at the time). So I gave them a quiz.

At the end, I asked everyone to pick up their papers, and when they did, I had them tear those papers into pieces. The lesson that day was to be careful what you wish for.

I did as many things like that as I could; I prided myself on teaching not just the facts of the assignment but life lessons, too.

I pulled inspiration from my favorite teacher and had my own Mikkelsen-isms, and I made sure to let the quiet kids know that class participation would be part of their grade. And I wrote little eights, nines, and tens next to their names when they spoke up.

When I started high school, I never did the reading, since I had never had to do any prep for class before Hunter. But now that I was a teacher, I read everything. I tore through Mrs. Acker's reading list so that I could be adept at leading discussions of the material, and so that I could give a pop quiz if I wanted to. I never wanted to—I am *not* an out-of-touch aristocrat.

I did, however, make the kids think on their feet. I even taught them improv by having them act out what would have happened if characters had made different decisions throughout the book. If you understand the characters in a book well enough to figure out what they'd do in a given situation, then you understand the book. And if you can grade students based on their interpretation of the characters, then you understand the book, too.

Teaching was a perfect fit for my nerd-based intellectual curiosity. Through the process of running a classroom, I completed the transformation into a serious student that had begun with Mr. Mikkelsen two years earlier. If you do the prep work, then the assignments are easy. That strategy transferred to my other classes, and I got ahead of my work in almost all of them. When you've actually done the reading, there's no need to avoid getting called on and no need to hem and haw your way through an answer. When you prepare, you just know the information you're being asked for. Before I did the reading ahead of time, I always thought the kids who knew the answers had magical powers.

How does he know all this? He's a witch! Burn him!

I took my responsibilities as a teacher seriously, and I took the students even more seriously. Even though I wasn't put together myself, I was more put together than the average freshman. I did what I could to help them with both their assignments and their out-of-class problems.

Toward the end of the year, I had a how-has-everything-been-going conversation with Mrs. Acker. I told her that while I was genuinely enjoying the work, I wondered about all of my added responsibilities. The further into the year I got, the more I realized that other interns were basically secretaries while I was teaching a class by myself.

"Why did you sign up for this internship?" Mrs. Acker asked me, with her usual smile.

"I thought I'd like teaching," I replied.

"And do you?" Mrs. Acker asked.

"Yes," I said. "Even more than I thought I would."

"And would you have learned that if all I had had you do was staple papers and collect exams?"

Touché, Mrs. Acker, touché. She went on to explain that when she failed to show up for class, it was purposeful, because I could never learn to be a teacher if I was doing it just to impress her for a good grade. She was ensuring I could swim by giving me the opportunity to sink. Mrs. Acker explained that there's no substitute for experience—and if I ever wanted to have a real shot at being a teacher, I needed to understand how teaching was really done.

I originally took the internship because I liked the idea of teaching, but also because I wanted to get out of taking one of my classes. In the end, I did way more work and learned way more than I ever would have done in a run-of-the-mill classroom. Damn it—Mrs. Acker tricked me into learning and enjoying learning.

As clever as I thought my little pop-quiz stunt was, Mrs. Acker was miles beyond me. Or she was using the class period to get high in her car. Hey, why not both?

PRESSING ON

ANOTHER GET-OUT-OF-CLASS-FREE OPPORTUNITY HUNTER
had for seniors was something called an ICY project. ICY stood
for inter-collegiate year, and the premise was that our senior
year wasn't just supposed to be for learning in a classroom but
also for learning for the world in general. I know, we were a
bunch of hippies.

Unlike teaching internships, an ICY project was something
that every student did. So I had to choose mine.

I assume the projects are way more organized and high-tech
now, but at the time, the ICY office had a stack of index cards,
each one with the name, company, and phone number of a previous ICY project. Those index cards were all we had to go on.
There were no reviews or recommendations, no warnings to
avoid a project because the boss was a jerk or encouragement
to try a project because the work was rewarding. Just a stack of
index cards with names, companies, and phone numbers.

I didn't know what I wanted to do with my life. I still didn't
have enough confidence to believe that I could pursue comedy as

a career, nor did anyone around me believe that would be viable. I'd have been taken more seriously if I had insisted I was going to pitch for the Mets than if I said I wanted to be a stand-up comedian. And that was after I gave up eight runs in a third of an inning.

I knew the two things I enjoyed most were sports and writing, though I hadn't ever thought to combine the two professionally. When I told the ICY counselor that I was interested in sports and writing, she also didn't think to combine the two. That makes sense. The ICY counselor was just a French teacher who spent a few hours a week handing students index cards.

The three index cards she handed me all had to do with sports or writing. The first card was an internship at the *New York Times*. As a New Yorker with hopes of being a journalist, there was no better place to work than the *New York Times*. The problem was that the ICY project was in the classifieds department. What a dream—I could file ads for used cars, just like Woodward and Bernstein.

It was the *New York Times*, though. And maybe I could make such an impression in classifieds that they'd bump me up to something really special, like obituaries. I called and left a message.

The second card was for a counselor position at the YMCA. That, I could get behind. Sure, it wouldn't help my career at all, but I could get school credit for teaching kids to play dodgeball. I enjoyed teaching Mrs. Acker's class, and I'd probably enjoy dodgeball even more. I called and left a message.

The third card was for an internship for Clement Sports. Kenneth Clement was a hockey writer with an office on the Upper West Side of Manhattan. The Upper West Side was a half hour bus ride from Hunter in the opposite direction from my Queens apartment. The potential annoyance of the commute alone discouraged me from applying; I knew that commute well from my days dating Colleen Barrett. But Clement Sports was writing, and it was sports. So I called and left a message.

For a few days, no one called back. I thought about seeing if Marvel still had an internship to offer; but I had long since lost Mary's number, and who knew if she even worked there anymore. As I contemplated trekking back to the Marvel offices in person, I finally got a call back. It was Kenneth Clement.

The call was quick—Kenneth seemed like a busy man who had hired many interns in the past and didn't want to waste time. He offered me the job without meeting me in person and demanded I make a decision while we were still on the phone. I said yes and told him that I would have to tell the other places I was interviewing that I was no longer available. I planned on telling them both that, if they ever called back.

On my first day working for Kenneth, I quickly learned why I didn't have an in-person interview. If I'd had an in-person interview, I may not have taken the job. Kenneth's office was in his home, in a creaky, prewar apartment building. Which war, I couldn't say for certain. Probably World War I. Possibly the Civil War. Maybe even the Hundred Years' War.

Parts of the office were exceedingly impressive. Kenneth had a collection of hockey media guides that dated back to before most teams were in the league. He also had walls and walls of books, many of which he had written. And newspapers. He had so many newspapers. The size of the apartment was also impressive—a four-bedroom apartment on the Upper West Side was not cheap. Though it was pretty easy to figure out that he'd been living there since the time that a four-bedroom apartment on the Upper West Side had been cheap. You could tell that just by reading the dates on the newspapers.

The least impressive thing about the office, other than the dust, was the ferret cage. Kenneth had two pet ferrets and part of the job of his interns was to clean up after them. Ferrets can be cute if you're looking at pictures of them. If you're cleaning their cages, ferrets are smelly weasels with a tendency to bite. I'd imagine it's hard to conduct a successful in-person interview when the whole office smells of ferret.

The first time I had to clean the ferret cage, I made the rookie mistake of thinking the ferrets wouldn't bolt the moment I opened the door. Thankfully, I was the only one in the office, so Kenneth didn't see me chasing two ferrets around a four-bedroom apartment. If the ferrets pooped before I caught them, at least there was newspaper everywhere.

I got used to the ferret smell after a while and got down to work, but I screwed up during my first week (and not just because I almost lost the ferrets). Before Kenneth left to cover a game, he told me to finish researching for a story he was working on. So I did and then headed home. What I didn't do is tell him where on the computer I had stored the completed files. While I was away for the weekend, visiting family and unreachable, Kenneth had to redo all of my work from the week because he couldn't find what I'd already done. I learned an important lesson about communication that day, as well as how to stare at the floor when your boss is yelling at you. I spent most of the next week on ferret duty. Yes, the pun is intentional.

Over the next few weeks, I got better at completing my job, and I started enjoying it, too. I mainly did research for Kenneth's books, but there were perks. One day, I had to go to the NHL's offices to pick up a packet of media clips that Kenneth needed for a story. Beaming with pride, I walked into the NHL's office and picked up an envelope—a job any bicycle courier would have found boring. But this was the office of a professional sports league. To me, that manila envelope was magic.

Kenneth began trusting me more and more and even let me contribute a few quips for a column he wrote for a newspaper in upstate New York. His column always ended with one-liner observations about sports (and occasionally about music for old people). Kenneth's one-liners were usually spot-on but fairly dry, so I started writing jokes. After the first few weeks of Kenneth using some of my work, he gave me space in his column, referring to me as his intrepid young reporter or other such terms usually found in Superman comics from the 1950s.

One day, Kenneth asked me if I wanted to go to a Knicks game. Of course I did—I'd only ever been to one Knicks game in my life; tickets were both expensive and difficult to come by. After I said yes, I thought of the awkwardness of sitting there for a whole game with a boss almost four times my age. Maybe we could pass the time by talking about the game. Or ferrets.

Before I could even finish worrying, Kenneth left me instructions on where to pick up my press pass. Whoa. Hold the rotary, wall-mounted phone. I was going as press?

I was going as press. By myself. At seventeen, I was technically too young to get a credential. But Kenneth had been working with Madison Square Garden so long, that rule didn't even matter. The Knicks's media department assumed I was eighteen, and when I got to the Garden, there was a credential waiting for me with my correctly spelled name on it. It could have said Dave Hoffmeyer; I'd have been just as excited.

If I thought the lobby of the NHL was impressive, you can imagine how I felt the first time I stepped into a professional locker room. I took copious notes during the game and stuck my recorder in the face of anyone who was talking. And, feeling bold, I even interviewed a few people who weren't talking until I asked them to.

While waiting for the players to finish showering and come out for interviews, I approached two celebrity fans. They were standing in the interview area, so I figured they were interested in being interviewed.

The first fan was New York Jets wide receiver and number one–overall draft pick Keyshawn Johnson. Johnson flatly (and rudely) turned me down, even going as far as to call me *kid*. And not in the endearing way that Superman said it to Jimmy Olsen.

Hurt but not broken, I walked over to *Hanging with Mr. Cooper* star Mark Curry, who couldn't have been more gracious. Mark gave me plenty for my story and was just a general pleasure to be around. Eight years later, I found myself opening for Mark at a comedy club in Atlanta. I told the crowd the story of meeting him and ended my set by saying that I learned two lessons that day.

"One," I said, "is be nice to everyone. You never know who is going to be introducing you in the future."

"Two," I continued, "Keyshawn Johnson is an asshole."

I wrote about the Knicks experience for Kenneth, who gave me half his column that week. The column did well, and Kenneth scheduled me to cover another Knicks game and a Rangers game. The word got around school pretty quickly that I was hobnobbing with (being ignored by) celebrities, and I was offered a column in my school paper, too. Suddenly, people who'd never cared what I had to say now voluntarily read it. Most of my classmates still ignored me, but I didn't mind. I was being ignored in the locker room by much more important people.

After some successful columns, I was offered a spot at the Columbia Scholastic Press Association's (CSPA) fall conference. CSPA is an organization that honors the best in high school journalism and offers seminars about every aspect of student journalism. I'd never heard of it until one of my editors asked me if I wanted to go. *Sure,* I thought. *Why the hell not.* The Kinnus turned out pretty great—I'd give this a try, too.

Columbia was a few blocks from Kenneth Clement's office, and I was already thinking about applying to Columbia for college. I didn't want to (read: was too scared to) leave New York, which mainly left me Columbia and NYU if I didn't want to go to a school in the city university system. Everyone in my family for three generations had gone to a city university, and I wanted to forge my own path.

Every senior at Hunter was given a college counselor, and I had drawn the short straw of Mrs. Vega. Students passed Mrs. Vega stories down every year; her ignorance was legend. There was the story where Mrs. Vega asked a student who got a perfect score on his SATs what his breakdown was. Or the story where Mrs. Vega recommended that a girl interested in Judaic studies forsake Brandeis for Notre Dame. I refused to believe those stories were true. How could anyone that oblivious be responsible for the future of such bright students? I don't know how it was true, but it was true.

The day I learned that you don't have to respect *all* your elders was the day I sat in Mrs. Vega's office and she insisted that I check out Northwestern University. I had told her I was interested in journalism, but I had also told her I didn't want to leave New York. Mrs. Vega made me promise I'd at least research

Northwestern, so I said yes, and she proceeded to look up Northwestern by searching for Chicago in a guide to American colleges. A guide that was divided by state.

Mrs. Vega flipped through rapidly, unable to find the listings for Chicago.

"Colorado. Delaware. Why can't I find Chicago?"

"Well," I said, holding back most of my laughter. "Chicago is not a state—Illinois is the state. But were Chicago a state, it would still not be located alphabetically between Colorado and Delaware."

Mrs. Vega asked me to promise not to tell anyone what had happened. I told her I wouldn't, knowing that I would absolutely tell everyone, if for no other reason than to prevent such a disgraceful screw-up from happening to anyone else. Years later I learned that her gaffe was even worse than I thought. Northwestern's main campus isn't even in Chicago. It's in Evanston.

The opening event for CSPA was in Low Library Rotunda, the same space at Columbia where Pulitzer Prizes are awarded. I spent that day feeling wowed by everything I saw. I came back from CSPA and began my early-decision application. I knew where I wanted to spend the next four years of my life.

The idea that I wanted to go to Columbia, after I'd started high school so abysmally academically, was a little crazy. But between Mr. Mikkelsen teaching me the pride of knowing the work, Mrs. Acker showing me the value of being prepared, and

Kenneth Clement yelling at me about deadlines, my grades had been pulled up far enough that I had a shot. My SAT scores were great, and I had some pretty stellar extracurricular activities to include on the application, like improv, Brick Prison, softball, and the most prestigious and spectacularly impressive accomplishment of all, homecoming king.

Unfortunately, Columbia agreed that my applying there was a little crazy, and I was not accepted as an early decision. I also applied to NYU, Syracuse, Sarah Lawrence, Stony Brook, and Hunter College. I didn't particularly want to go to any of them, but I had to give myself options. And I applied to a second program at Columbia. Perhaps I should have considered Northwestern, too. I've always loved the great state of Chicago.

The stress of waiting to find out where you're accepted to college (or whether you're accepted at all) is not something I would wish on anyone, even though everyone who applies to college has to go through it. Where you go to college can change the direction of your life in countless ways—from meeting a new group of friends to falling in love to walking into career opportunities, college is extremely important. And everyone just has to sit around and wait for months until they learn what the rest of their life is going to look like. At least I got to go to Knicks games in the meantime.

There's a movie called *Sliding Doors* that explores the idea that the simple act of missing a train could have a tremendous effect on your life. I often think about how different my life would be had the snowstorm not led me to USY. Or if the *New York Times* or the YMCA had called me back first. Or if I hadn't agreed to go to the Columbia Scholastic Press Association. Or if I'd ever actually seen *Sliding Doors* instead of just figuring out the plot from seeing a few commercials.

Here's a sentence no one else has ever said—cleaning up after those ferrets was life-changing.

THE DAY
THAT WAS TEN
MINUTES LONG

IT HAD BEEN YEARS SINCE I JOINED THE IMPROV CLUB.
I'd been in a few hundred scenes, killing some and bombing others but always trying to learn how I could get better.

One particularly memorable bomb was the time I tried anti-comedy. A game of questions was taking place in a proctologist's office, and my scene partner started by asking, "Do you come here often?"

I responded by asking, "What are you trying to get me to do, play some sort of improv game?" I thought it was a creative way to push the form of the game. But it went over as well as "Frankly, Scarlet."

Through my successes and failures, one thing I hadn't done was perform improv in front of anyone who wasn't in the improv club. I don't count that day I did improv in USY, or my time in Brick.

As well as those performances had gone, there is a difference between building a scene and having a scene built for you. And I did not have a leading role in those productions; I was just a brief cameo in someone else's improv group.

Occasionally, we'd have visitors during our lunch meetings. Sometimes my copresident, Paulina, had a friend swing by, but I didn't count those occasions since that friend was Rebecca Chaikin.

Despite how much the improv club practiced, we never thought to go public. But Paulina was friends with the class president's girlfriend, Cathy, and Cathy asked Paulina if we wanted to participate in Arts Day. Arts Day was an annual assembly where students and faculty showcased the creative side of Hunter. It was the Freak Hallway's day to shine. Well, not a full day—Arts Day was only an hour long.

The events were pretty standard year after year: The Asian American Alliance performed a traditional dance. The music class played something on strings. And Hunter's resident student R&B group, Dujeous, closed and brought down the house. The problem was that most members of Dujeous had graduated the year prior. So Cathy was left with a slot to fill.

When Paulina brought the idea to us, the club was a mix of thrilled and terrified. It was one thing to do these games in front of each other—it was another thing entirely to try them in front of an audience. We were afraid that the audience would be filled with people who didn't appreciate good improv. In other words, an audience that didn't get our inside jokes.

With any improv troupe, punch lines can often become a string of private jokes. Scenes can become references to specific improvisers—or worse yet, references to jokes from previous scenes. Private jokes are a ton of fun when you're just messing around. But they're terrible traps to fall into when you're performing for strangers—or worse yet, people you know personally, but who don't get your references. People you know personally who don't get your references and whom you have to spend the next few months with.

"Wait a minute," one of the students said. "Arts Day is next week!"

As the club started freaking out about whether we'd be prepared or not, I spoke up.

"Why do we need to prepare?" I asked. "It's improv."

All we really needed to do was to choose the game that we'd play and the people who would play it. We decided that the players would be the three seniors. We were the oldest, we were the most experienced, and we were the ones who got to choose who represented the group. That was settled, so it was time to choose the game.

World's Worst was high risk–high reward. The audience shouts out a profession, and three people take turns acting as if they're part of that profession. So if they shout "gynecologist," we take turns saying things like, "Has anyone seen my ring?" World's Worst is all one-liners, so a good joke hits incredibly hard, but it's very easy to misfire.

Superheroes is longer-form improv, where each actor is given a useless superpower and everyone has to build a scene together as they try to save the city. So, the Girl With No Hair finds a creative way to use her bald head against her enemies, and the Guy with Two-Dimensional Vision creates the physical comedy of feeling around until he's caressing his colleague's bald head. The problem with Superheroes is that it takes a while to build the scene, and we didn't have an audience willing to give us leeway. Performing comedy for a crowd that didn't intend to see you perform is a tough proposition. We had to get their attention quickly.

We settled on Party Quirks, a game that can impress crowds both with comedy and with a player's ability to read the scene. Three guests are given strange quirks (like Superheroes), and the host of the party has to guess what those quirks are. So the guy that thinks all food is too hot starts freaking out about the salsa, but then also about how spicy the water is.

Party Quirks also comes with a great deal of audience participation because the crowd suggests the quirks, and they all know what the quirks are, but the host doesn't. It creates a very fun vibe of people wanting to yell at the host when the host doesn't guess quickly enough. And people are extremely impressed when the host nails it immediately.

We added a junior as our fourth player, and I was picked as the party host. I'd played the Party Quirks host a hundred times in our little classroom and rarely got stumped. This was my best game.

Arts Day came, and after a traditional dance for Chinese New Year and a cello performance, it was our turn. I was taken outside the auditorium while the rules were explained to the crowd, and then I was brought in to host the party. The irony of me hosting a party was not lost on me.

The quirks were easy, and I guessed all three of them right in all three games. If anything, we went too quickly—the hints came too fast and my guesses came too quickly. We were so intent on impressing everyone, we didn't allow the scene time to breathe.

But it worked. It worked so well that some people asked us if we'd planted the quirks in the crowd. That is the mark of a good improv performance—when people assume it's so good that it had to have been planned ahead.

Our lives didn't change because of that performance. After that week, no one mentioned it again. But Arts Day showed me that I could handle myself in front of a real crowd, and it showed me that I was no longer scared of attention. I'd come a long way from the kid who refused to speak in economics class.

I STOLE A PIMP

CARNIVAL ALWAYS SIGNIFIED THE HOME STRETCH OF
the school year. When I was a senior, Carnival signified the
home stretch of my entire high school career.

Even when I was in grade school, I dreaded most schoolwide events. The problem with schoolwide events was that they
required money. Every extra dollar I made babysitting was spent
on clothing or food or other such silly luxuries. I hated book
fairs and bake sales because I could never afford to buy anything,
and the funnel cake at Carnival was usually no different.

I've referenced my lack of money a fair amount in this book,
and I want to be clear—we weren't starving, but sometimes I was
hungry. I was lucky that we had enough money to always have
food on the table, though it was often canned tuna purchased
with coupons. I had clothes on my back and a roof over my head,
but the idea of being able to spend money on funnel cake was as
alien to me as how funnel cake is made in the first place.

Senior year, Carnival was actually different. I had the usual
frustration of not being able to participate in the booths or go

outside without having to slather myself in SPF infinity. But that was muted by the excitement of high school finally winding down. I could see the light at the end of the teenage tunnel. And I was okay. I'd found my friends, I'd shaped up academically, and Theo Webster never hurt me (other than emotionally).

Part of Carnival involved the juniors unveiling their mascot. Instead of the school having one mascot for everyone, each grade had their own. I know that's an odd tradition, but we didn't have a homecoming game, so we had to invent our traditions where we could.

Hunter mascots were always animals named with terrible puns. Ours was Karate Squid, which thankfully beat out Periodic Table of the Elephants. Karate Squid also beat out many other possibilities I don't remember—only Periodic Table of the Elephants was dumb enough to stick with me.

The junior mascot was Chimp Daddy and some of the students made a prototype by taking a giant doll and dressing it up in a fur coat and pink hat. After the pimp doll was carted off, everyone pretty much forgot about it because hey, funnel cake.

Despite my lack of desserts, I sat on the school steps in a pretty good mood. All that changed when Ozzie gave me the "good" news.

"You know," Ozzie said, "Alexa Howard doesn't hate you."

"Well then she's a fantastic actress," I replied, laughing.

"She is," Ozzie said. "She told me."

I stopped laughing. I was more confused than anything. I

demanded Ozzie explain what he meant, since I knew Alexa had been unsuccessfully hitting on him for the last few months and he was privy to information. Ozzie had no interest in Alexa—he knew just how terrible she had been to me. But Ozzie rejecting her advances hadn't stopped Alexa from trying. And the most recent time she tried to pique his interest was that morning at Carnival, where she confessed to him that she actually had no problem with me.

"Steve's a pretty good guy," Alexa told Ozzie. "I see how he is with the team. He works hard, and he cares about us. But I couldn't start being nice to him. What would people think? I have to keep up appearances."

What would people think? That she'd matured like the rest of us had? That she wasn't pure evil? That sometimes humans can change their minds about one another?

Normally, I'd be happy to learn that someone who'd disliked me for years had changed her mind. But I couldn't get past why she had treated me so poorly, for years, in the first place.

She had been putting me through garbage because she thought it made her look better. I don't know why she thought that—perhaps because being kind to me would have made her look soft. It didn't make sense to me, but this was much worse than her just being mean to me because she hated me. The remarks she had for me, the names she called me, the academic sabotage —she put me through all that just because she wanted to look cool. Ozzie was wrong about this being good news. This was very, very angry news.

As I stewed in my anger and wished I could silence it with funnel cake, I was given an opportunity. One of the Dans came over to tell us that the juniors had officially been given control of the senior class president's office, and that was where they were keeping the pimp doll. Dan then asked if anyone would come with him to try to break in.

Normally, I wouldn't have said yes to breaking in to anything. It's infantile and risky and doesn't have much upside. But I was angry and hungry, and I wanted a victory.

"I'm in," I told Dan, knowing full well it was idiotic.

I had a theory—we had keys to the newspaper office, which shared a wall with the senior class president's office. And in that part of the school, the walls didn't go all the way up to the ceiling. More importantly, the ceiling tiles were removable. When you spend years hiding in the nurse's office staring at the ceiling, you learn a few things.

I climbed on a desk and entered the ceiling. I'd seen enough spy movies to know to carefully lower myself and not put any weight on anything that wasn't completely solid. But unlike in spy movies, there was no red laser to avoid or alarm to trip. Getting up over that wall was easier than any of us expected.

I got a few small scratches on my forearm, but I successfully went over the wall, replaced the ceiling tiles, picked up the doll, and walked out the door of the senior class president's office without issue. Dan told me I should have climbed back over since there was no way to lock the door from the outside without a key. And that is why I walked out the door instead. It wasn't due to an unwillingness to climb back over; I wanted the juniors to think that their mascot vanished because they had accidentally left their office unlocked. I'd never stopped enjoying a good prank.

We waited until most people had left for the day before hiding the doll in a garbage bag and walking him out of the newspaper office. We had the entire weekend to plan what we'd do with Chimp Daddy. When most people steal a mascot, the big reveal is, *Ha ha, we stole your mascot.* We wanted something better.

Hunter had a wall at the edge of the courtyard with a few "windows" in it that had been part of an old armory. It was just a red brick wall, not connected to a building, and the windows had bars but no glass. If you can picture that, now you understand why our theater company was called Brick Prison.

Our plan was to show up early Monday and string up the doll on the side of that wall holding a sign that said, WHO'S YOUR DADDY? Even now, I look back and still believe that was a perfect way to reveal what we'd done. The only problem was that getting the doll up there was much harder than climbing into the office.

There were six of us, so we stationed three students on each side of the wall. We tied the doll to a tennis ball on a long string, and threw the tennis ball through the window. Or we tried to, anyway. Getting a tennis ball through a third story window covered in bars wasn't easy.

Wild as my arm was, I did have an arm, so it was my job to get that ball through that window. It took several throws but I finally succeeded. As the doll was being hoisted by the three on the outside of the building, it was suddenly dropped. Those of us on the inside heard the guys on the outside loudly say, "no, it's just us." We didn't know what was happening, but we knew it couldn't be good. There was no sense in all six of us getting caught, so the three of us on the inside ran.

It wasn't until later that day that we learned what had happened. The rumors of Dr. Haanraats jogging around Hunter at five A.M. were true, and he saw three students using a pulley system to hoist something onto the side of the school. Instead of being proud that they were using something they had learned in physics class, Dr. Haanraats suspended all three of them for theft.

I've already made it clear that I thought Dr. Haanraats was a terrible school administrator, but those suspensions cemented it. Suspension was beyond a harsh punishment for a harmless prank, and pranks were a senior-class tradition at Hunter. The doll wasn't damaged, and the juniors would be getting their pimp back as soon as they got to school. Sure, we all deserved punishment, starting with a phone call to our parents (though with Brent, calling his parents would be difficult). But what we didn't deserve was a potential black mark on our futures, particularly when this level of punishment was unprecedented for previous, similar pranks. Phillip pulling a knife on me twice was fine, but playfully hoisting up a toy in the context of a school-encouraged rivalry—that demanded severe punishment.

I wasn't suspended, but only because Hunter never knew I had anything to do with it. The three of us on the inside of the wall got away, and those on the outside swore they were the only ones that were involved, and they weren't pressed any further. Clearly Dr. Haanraats had never done the build-a-pulley physics assignment. I never took physics and even I knew you needed someone on both sides of the wall to make this work.

The three who got caught saw no benefit to turning the rest of us in. Their punishment was no harsher than it would have been had there been more of us, so they just accepted their fate and protected us. I was amazed that I had friends willing to do that for me.

Dr. Haanraats never found out I was involved, but the rest of my class did, and I showed off my scratches as battle scars. While we didn't get the picture we wanted of the mascot up on the wall, we were heroes for trying.

PAPA WAS A ROLLING STONE

UNLESS YOU COUNT MY BUNK AT RAMAH, I ONLY EVER knew one home until I was fifteen. And then Forest Hills became my second.

I loved it. Forest Hills was the most upscale part of Queens, and upscale was something I didn't normally get to be around. I loved walking up and down Austin Street and going into stores, even though I couldn't afford to buy anything. Jacob and I knew every inch of those streets. We knew the staff of the pool hall and played pool before we were legally allowed. We made friends with the clerks at McDonalds, and they told us that if you filled out a survey card, you could get a free order of fries (which we did every time we were hungry). We even said hi to the homeless guys, who also said hi to us. We were part of the neighborhood. Then one day, I wasn't anymore.

At the time, if you sold a property for profit and didn't buy another within two years, you got hit by a massive capital gains tax. We'd lived in Forest Hills for two years, so my mother was faced with a problem—buy something else now or lose the money to taxes and the opportunity to ever buy in the future. We could not afford to buy a place in Forest Hills. We could barely afford to rent a place in Forest Hills, and that was with four of us living in a two-bedroom apartment. So we moved.

As our time in Forest Hills was ending, David got married and moved out. I had only a few months before graduation, and I was pretty sure I was going to a school where I didn't have to live at home. But for the time being, we all still needed places to sleep, so my mother looked for small apartments one neighborhood over, in Rego Park.

For every upscale neighborhood, there are people who keep the neighborhood running. Clerks at the stores and servers at the restaurants. The housekeepers and cab drivers and garbagemen and cops who all work in Forest Hills—they don't live in Forest Hills. They live in Rego Park.

In addition to simply being a much less expensive alternative to Forest Hills, Rego Park is also an old-immigrant neighborhood. When I say old immigrants, I mean World War II immigrants. The people who lived in Rego Park were not children and grandchildren of the people who'd moved here from Europe. Those children and grandchildren grew up and moved to places like Forest Hills. When I say Rego Park is an old-immigrant neighborhood, I mean most of my neighbors were old immigrants.

My mother found a first-floor apartment that was technically on the second floor because the complex was on a hill. The apartment was a small two-bedroom, so my mother built a temporary wall in the master bedroom to give Beth and I enough space for a bed and a dresser each. I gave Beth the slightly bigger part of the room, since she was commuting to a city college and I had every intention of leaving Rego Park as soon as I was able.

As my mother was in the process of apartment hunting, I was still waiting to hear back from Columbia. I did, however, begin hearing from other schools.

I was accepted into Hunter College, though I had no intention of ever accepting their acceptance. I'd applied because I needed to have a school on the list that was cheap enough that I could afford to go if I didn't get any scholarships or financial aid anywhere else. My high school's full name is Hunter College High School because it is administered by Hunter College. Because of that relationship, Hunter High School students are able to take classes at Hunter College. I'd been to Hunter College many times, and I had no interest in making the relationship permanent.

I was also accepted to Stony Brook, a state college in New York that is fondly referred to as Stoner Brook. It wasn't my top choice, but I'd have been okay with it. Hey, Mrs. Acker was often stoned, and she was great.

The next letter came from Sarah Lawrence and was also a yes. I had mainly applied to Sarah Lawrence because they'd rejected my brother, David, and I wanted to see if they'd accept me. I know that is extremely petty, but there's something to be said for academically surpassing the guy who jokingly called you stupid most of your life.

I was still waiting on my big three. Columbia, NYU, and Syracuse. I didn't particularly want to go to college upstate, but Syracuse has an excellent journalism program and their mascot has red hair, too. Syracuse accepted me and gave me their highest possible journalism scholarship, which actually made it affordable. They were very impressed by my sportswriting internship (though they didn't comment on what they'd thought of my winning homecoming king). The only problem was that Syracuse gave me a deadline to respond, and it was right around when I was supposed to hear back from Columbia and NYU. How could I respond to Syracuse before hearing back from my top two choices? I didn't want to play my hand before I knew what all my cards were.

NYU came back a few days before Syracuse's deadline. While I was accepted, the financial aid just wasn't there. At the time, NYU was the most expensive college in the country, and without a scholarship, I could barely have afforded textbooks. With NYU ruled out, I started considering whether I'd go to Syracuse, Sarah Lawrence, or Stony Brook. Columbia was both a long shot and expensive, and I still hadn't heard from them.

My mother called Syracuse to ask them to extend their scholarship deadline. "If you want him enough that you'll offer a scholarship, why can't you wait one more week?" There was something hilarious about my mother pleading with someone to be irresponsible about their deadlines. But it also made me feel great to see her fight for me like that. It didn't make me feel great to see her lose. I had to make a choice—accept Syracuse right then or gamble on Columbia. I don't know why, but I gambled.

I just couldn't imagine committing to Syracuse only to find out I'd gotten into to Columbia a few days later. Though I was also terrified of refusing Syracuse only to find out I'd gotten rejected from Columbia a few days later. I imagined showing up on Syracuse's front steps pleading with them to take me back.

"Baby," I'd say, from behind a huge bouquet of orange flowers. "You're the only college for me!"

Meanwhile, Jacob bet me ten dollars I'd be accepted into Columbia. It was a good bet to take—if I was accepted, I'd be so happy that losing ten dollars would be fine. And if I was rejected, hey, at least I'd get ten dollars to offset the sadness a bit. It didn't.

The day I got that rejection letter from Columbia was an extremely tough day. It was tough enough that I was still sad the next morning. So when I got to school, I decided to just leave. I took the ten dollars I'd won from Jacob, and I went to a movie. For all the time I'd spent in the nurse's office, I'd never actually skipped a full day of school before. I didn't know what would happen—would my parents get a phone call? Or would the school not even notice? Maybe I was just in the nurse's office the whole day and not a movie theater on Eighty-sixth Street.

For most of my life, the thing that kept me from getting into trouble was the generic fear of trouble, even without the knowledge of what trouble actually looked like. Fear of the unknown was also the reason Theo terrorized me so easily. But at this point, I didn't care. Whatever trouble was, I would face it. My dream of going to Columbia had been crushed. I was entitled to see a movie.

When I got home that day, my mother didn't ask how school was, which was out of character for her. Did she know about the movie? Was there a system in place to catch kids skipping school? Trouble had arrived. I didn't know what form it would take, but it was happening.

"Go look at the dining room table," my mother said, as if we had a separate dining room and not just a table in a corner of the living room. I did, cautiously, half expecting to find Dr. Haanraats hiding beneath it.

There was a letter on the table from Columbia. I'd been accepted.

It took me a while to process this—how the hell was this possible? Was the letter I'd received the day before a mistake? A mistake could happen. Earlier that year, I'd received consecutive letters accepting me and then rejecting me from a school I hadn't even applied to due to a clerical error. When that happened, it was hilarious, since it was a school I'd have never attended in the first place. But this wasn't funny. This was serious.

I read the letter carefully, trying to bury the conflicting emotions of fear, excitement, and confusion. And I understood. I had applied to both Columbia College and the School of General

Studies at Columbia, and I'd assumed that I'd been rejected from both when I'd gotten the first letter. But that first letter was only for Columbia College. Not only did I get in to the School of General Studies, but I was going to receive enough financial aid to make it feasible. Though I would need twenty bucks more, since clearly I had to concede loss in the bet with Jacob.

We moved to Rego Park soon after that, and I didn't mind the tiny room and that my ancient neighbors would constantly be yelling at me in Russian (what's the Russian word for *young whippersnapper*?). I didn't mind Rego Park because I knew I had an exit strategy. In just a few more months, I'd be going to Columbia to be a writer.

Jacob got in to his first choice of colleges, too—Johns Hopkins in Baltimore. Ozzie would be going to Villanova, Rebecca had gotten in to the University of Rhode Island, Mason would be attending the University of Maryland, and Randy was headed to Cornell. All the time I'd spent in high school trying to figure out who I was and how I fit in (or if I even should fit in) was coming to an end. But for now, I still had some friends to face life with.

THAT TIME
I KILLED TWO
PEOPLE

TO UNDERSTAND KILLER IS TO UNDERSTAND HUNTER.

Killer is a game where teams of six students try to kill each other using toy guns. In my time at Hunter, it cost ten dollars to play, and the winning team split the almost two thousand dollars of entry fees. It had been outlawed by the administration as far back as the 1980s, and possibly earlier. Every year, students skipped school to stake out each other's houses. Every year, someone almost got hit by a car (or did get hit). Every year anyone caught playing was immediately suspended and banned from prom and walking at graduation. And every year, hundreds of students played anyway.

That was the essence of Hunter. A bunch of kids too smart for their own good who didn't respect authority when it didn't make sense. Outlawing Killer made us want to play more and made the game more intense. Banning it wasn't the answer. I don't know what would have been, but banning it only made Killer grow in popularity.

Teams were pitted against each other in a wheel—so you had two teams coming for you at all times. As teams were eliminated, the wheel shrank and you were given new opponents until there was just one team left, or two weeks had passed. The guns were tracer guns (sometimes called disc guns), and the bullets were little plastic disks that looked like the middle of an old record album. Every now and then when I see a tracer on the ground in a park somewhere, I smile, thinking of Killer.

There were rules that kept us relatively safe. Not physically safe (you were never physically safe while playing Killer), but safe from getting caught. The main rule was that you couldn't kill anyone on school grounds. So for two weeks, people would bring their lunch to school and find creative ways to sneak on and off the property. Once you had two feet off the school block, it was open season.

I saw some of my classmates do some pretty amazing things. One slid across the hood of a parked car as he shot his target. Another threw a giant piece of poster board in the air to block a shot coming at him, and shot his target as the poster board fell. If anyone is ever looking for an amazing documentary subject, I'd recommend Killer.

Buying modified guns from students who'd graduated the year before was a tradition among the rich kids. But I barely had the ten-dollar registration fee and the eight dollars it cost to buy two regular guns in the first place, so I used my nerdiness and my father's engineering knowledge (i.e., *his* nerdiness) to open up my two guns and modify them myself. We adjusted the spring to make the guns shoot farther and faster and added washers on the outside for stability. My guns could shoot twice as fast and twice as far as any nonmodified guns. My guns were badass.

The first few days of the game were relatively dull for me. No one but Jacob knew my new Rego Park address, so I wasn't afraid of anyone staking out my apartment. Staking out really was a thing people did, and it was something I did the first day of Killer, too. Unfortunately, the enemy we were staking out was doing the same to someone else, so eventually we all just went to school.

I had one brief run-in with the law (i.e., a teacher). I was charging out of the basement doors after an opponent, who had his gun out ready to shoot as soon as we stepped off the block. As we got out of the doors, we almost bowled over a teacher. We were sure that we were caught, and both my opponent and I looked up at the teacher sheepishly. The teacher was our health teacher, sneaking a cigarette. We made eye contact—and with a mutual, I-won't-tell-anyone-if-you-don't-tell-anyone nod, we all went back inside.

Finally, a week in, someone found my address. I don't know how—Jacob was a teammate, so it certainly wasn't through him.

Killer was played with enough intensity that someone probably looked up a public record of my mother's that had our address on it. Maybe they bribed the mayor. However he got my address, a student named Kunal showed up at my apartment door.

My mother had been in the process of replacing the peephole on our door, because something in our lives was always broken, and we were always in the process of fixing it. Nothing was ever just fixed—it was always in process. These processes lasted for weeks, months, sometimes even years. Even my parents' marriage took years to finally be replaced with a divorce. This particular peephole process had been going on since we'd moved in.

Hearing someone outside my apartment, I peeled back a sliver of the duct tape that covered the object formerly known as peephole and saw Kunal trying to figure out what to do. He noticed the light and started yelling through the door.

"Come on, Steve! You can't stay in there forever." Which was a stupid thing for someone in a hallway to yell at someone in his own apartment. But he was right, sort of—I couldn't stay in there if I wanted to record a kill. And I did want that. I wanted to record a kill badly. Recording a kill got you respect. At this point, half my six-man team was already dead and we had zero kills among us. I could hide, but we were a week into Killer already, and I was tired of playing defense.

I could get out of the apartment if I wanted to. Our windows had grates on them, so I could grab one, lower myself, and drop down to the street. I could then walk through my own front door and blindside Kunal. It was perfect—I just had to figure out a way to keep Kunal at the door.

I thought of using the mini recorder I had from covering Knicks games to play a tape of my voice like it was *Ferris Bueller's Day Off*, but I quickly realized no one would fall for that. As I searched for another solution, my mother came home and saw Kunal in the hall, stalking the door. As my mother demanded an explanation, I took my chance. I swung the door open, dropped to the ground, and shot up. Kunal was hit before he even knew what was happening. Risk reaps reward. Kunal wasn't happy, but all is fair in love and war.

Word got out at school the next day that I'd recorded a kill at my own front door, and at first people were pleasantly surprised. I got words of congratulations and pats on the shoulder as people walked by. And then word got around that my mother had helped me. My mother had most certainly not helped me— at least not purposely. At worst, she was an unwitting human shield. Still, moms are killers of Killer. She may as well have called everyone in Queens and asked them to ride the bus with me again.

Later that day, another teammate of mine was taken out and the focus shifted away from my mother. Now, I had only one teammate left alive.

Every year, Hunter has a three-day trip to Washington, DC, for some of the seniors taking government classes. It's called Washington Seminar or more frequently Wash Sem because most people believe that shortening words makes you cool. I find that to be infuri.

The rules of Killer stated that people on Wash Sem couldn't kill each other. Sure, some of us jumped over cars, but you don't take a toy gun through a metal detector. Even *we* knew better than that.

The rules of Killer said nothing about non–Wash Sem people not being able to kill those who were on the trip. Wash Sem kills by non–Wash Sem people weren't explicitly outlawed because no one was crazy enough to try. We were New Yorkers—most of us didn't have cars or even driver's licenses. How the hell could any of us get to DC if we weren't on that school-sanctioned trip?

That night, I was talking to Nick about how our time in Killer was basically over. Nick was inexplicably my only teammate left standing. In a fit of impulsivity, I said, "We should go to DC tomorrow." Because Nick is Nick, he agreed.

We decided we'd skip school, something I had only ever done once before but Nick was intimately familiar with, and meet at the Port Authority Bus Station. The last time I skipped school to see a movie, I got into Columbia. Maybe this time I'd be elected senator.

I'd never taken a Greyhound before and I'd never been farther from New York than Baltimore. While DC is not much farther than Baltimore, this bus trip was a pretty crazy idea. I got to Port Authority first and bought my ticket while I waited for Nick. He was about fifteen minutes late—because he'd gotten killed on the way to meeting me.

Going to DC suddenly went from a dumb idea to an impossible idea. I had two opponents at Wash Sem—how could I possibly shoot them both by myself? They might have their guns on them (we always had our guns on us), and it would be very hard to shoot one without the other seeing. Or, much worse, without being caught by a teacher.

But I'd spent all the babysitting money I'd had on that ticket. I told Nick that if he came with me, I'd still go. He could help keep a lookout, and if I got caught, well, I would be a legend for trying. I liked the feeling I'd gotten when I climbed through that ceiling to take the mascot. And I wanted it again.

That was the shortest five-hour bus ride in history. We were excited for the sheer madness of what lay ahead. And we had to make plans. How were we going to ever find Wash Sem? Sure, we'd go to the area of DC with all the government buildings, but then what? Neither Nick nor I had ever been to DC before. We'd have to be smart about this. We'd have to be smart about our extremely stupid plan.

When we got to Washington, DC, I found a pay phone and called Hunter pretending to be the secretary of Joe J.'s father. I allegedly had an urgent message to get to Joe, so I was hoping the school could put me in touch. The person who answered told me the name of the hotel the students were staying at, but I knew we couldn't just wait at the hotel all day and still get back to New York at a reasonable hour. I tried again.

"Is there any way I could get it to Joe sooner?" I asked, almost calling him "Joe J." out of habit. "Do you have an itinerary? I don't mean to trouble you, but it's of the utmost importance."

I figured utmost importance is something important people say. And the teacher who'd answered the phone bought my act.

"I'm sorry," the teacher said. "It's not like we can get a message to him at the Department of Education."

I laughed, said "of course not," hung up, and told Nick we were headed to the Department of Education.

When Nick and I arrived, the school busses were out front, and we knew we had our opponents cornered. Just to make sure, I walked into the lobby and asked the guard if the tour from Hunter had left yet. She told me it hadn't, and I thanked her profusely while I explained that I'd missed the bus from the hotel and just wanted to catch up with them. She offered to radio to the tour, and I politely declined, explaining that I'd feel so guilty bothering them, it was my fault, and I would just wait patiently outside. I left, proud of my quick lie, ironically knowing that the guard admired my honesty.

I also left knowing for sure that no one went in or out of that building without going through a metal detector first. My opponents would be completely unsuspecting and completely unarmed.

The difficult part would be to kill two people by myself without any teachers seeing. I figured I'd use the other students on the trip as witnesses. Every student at Hunter, regardless of whether they played or not, respected the tradition of Killer. I knew no one would rat me out. When Wash Sem emerged from the building, I popped up from behind the stairs and shot Joe J. in the back so that he wouldn't see what happened, but other people would. I did not wanting him alerting his teammate.

Once Joe J. was dead (whether he knew it or not), I ran up to my other opponent, tapped him on the shoulder so he would definitely see me, plugged him in the chest, and ran as fast as I could away so that none of the teachers could see what happened. All I heard behind me was him cursing and the rest of the students laughing as Nick and I got around the block as fast as we could.

We'd done it. Our completely foolhardy mission had actually worked. Nick and I had a few hours to spare before we needed to catch another bus, so we walked around DC on that beautiful spring day, looking at the monuments to America's forefathers and feeling a little revolutionary ourselves.

By the time we got back to New York, word had already spread. People were surprised when I danced at junior prom, when I stole the mascot, and when I recorded my first kill. But this was outright shock. This was the quiet kid that had been a nonentity for so many years pulling off something that no one had ever even thought to do. This was me, for the first time, being cool.

I died the next day. After school, two of my opponents showed up at my apartment to take me out; I had gotten three kills and was the only one on my team preventing the wheel from getting smaller. I thought of climbing out the window and ambushing them, but before I could, they figured out something Kunal hadn't—that they could peel the duct tape back, too. They opened up the peephole and rained tracers upon me. At first, it was tough to admit it was over. I never saw or felt a tracer actually hit me, and I had had so much fun with the game that I wanted to keep playing until the end. But I must have been hit, and I was tired. I agreed to the kill, and my game was over. As they say, you can't win them all.

I knew Killer was just a silly game, but I was really proud of how I played. I racked up my three kills because I wasn't afraid. I could have let the feeling of defeat stop me before I ever went to DC. Instead, I pressed on and achieved one of the silliest victories of my life. Recording those kills in DC is my "I threw four touchdowns in a single game" glory-days story that I'll have forever—even if, in the end, I did get shot through a peephole. That was just one more thing ruined by my mother's penchant for procrastination.

When I got to college, we played a version of Killer called Assassins. The game was also supposed to last two weeks, but I won the whole thing in three days. They say high school prepares you for college. Sometimes, they are right.

KEEP IN TOUCH!

I WAS NEVER A FAN OF THE HUNTER YEARBOOK, MAINLY because every year, the "cool" kids ran it. Ours was run by The Clique, and the years before us were just run by the Cliques of other grades.

The yearbook often took cheap shots at people for their looks, because that's what the cool kids found to be cool. Even as a teenager I knew that comedy was best when it involved punching up and not down.

My first tangle with the yearbook came as a sophomore, when one of the photographers snapped a picture of me to use in a Separated-at-Birth feature. The joke was that I was so pale, I was separated at birth from a piece of paper. The only thing is, the writer was dumb enough to use a picture of a piece of loose leaf paper; so the joke fell flat enough that it was cut from the final version of the yearbook. I would have triumphantly said, "Go find someone else to make fun of!", but they were already too busy finding someone else to make fun of.

The other yearbook tradition that was tough was the ads.

Each senior got a free half-page with our picture and a few quotes, but most of the book was taken up by purchased ads. The rich families bought full pages to congratulate their children on their graduation, and the rich kids also bought pages to congratulate each other. Sometimes couples took out ads, which I imagine became particularly funny after they had broken up by Thanksgiving.

"You know all that stuff I said about 'eternal love' in the yearbook?" she'd say to him on a hurried phone call. "Well, you go to college across the country, and there is this guy on my floor who has a pet rabbit . . ."

I kept my page simple—one picture and one quote: "Love is the most important thing in life, but baseball is pretty good, too."

I was supposed to have four appearances in the yearbook—my mandatory half-page and group pictures on the clubs pages for softball, Brick Prison, and improv. I assumed that I wouldn't be part of an ad because I couldn't afford to contribute to one. I had no idea that the choice was out of my hands—and not for reasons involving money.

One Monday, Randy and Ozzie pulled Jacob and I aside to tell us that our group of friends had gotten together over the weekend and taken pictures for a yearbook ad without us. What was worse was that Randy and Ozzie were just invited to hang without being told why, because everyone knew that they would tell us. Our exclusion wasn't just an oversight. It was on purpose.

Ozzie tried to make me feel better, reminding me of the

expense of yearbook ads and saying that Jacob and I just weren't as close with some of the group as they were. He was right about both, but that didn't make our exclusion feel any better. Jacob and I were hurt, and we had every right to be.

That day, I went to Jacob's apartment after school, and it was impossible to keep our frustration a secret from his mother. We were angry, and we were betrayed. We felt that just when we had finally gotten comfortable at school, the rug had been pulled out from under us.

I'd felt this way before—when I lost the USY election. It was the realization that some of my friends weren't who I thought they were. Some of them weren't my friends at all.

"Why don't we just get your own ad?" Jacob's mother asked. "Show those boys how much fun you have without them?"

We tried to explain how expensive an ad was, and how it would look silly if we got one-eighth of a page compared to their full page. We tried to explain how our anger was about much more than the ad. And in our condescension to her, we hadn't realized that Jacob's mother was generously offering to pay for it.

Jacob's mother already knew why we were upset. She was suggesting that we didn't have to wallow in our anger—instead we could turn the yearbook into something we could have fun with. So we did.

As Jacob and I discussed ideas for the ad, just the two of us together in the yearbook began to make sense. Jacob had been there for me since the beginning, and I had been there for him.

We laid out a page with baseballs and guitars and our favorite quotes from A Tribe Called Quest. We had a lot of fun getting that page together.

The realization that the rest of the group didn't care about me like I thought they did didn't matter as much anymore. I still had Jacob as a close friend—and Randy and Ozzie were good enough friends to tell us what happened and stick up for us, even if their defense hadn't worked. Being left out of the yearbook ad cemented the lesson I'd learned in USY the previous year. I didn't need a dozen casual friends. I had a few close ones, and that's what mattered.

By the time the rest of the guys apologized, Jacob and I weren't even upset anymore.

"No hard feelings," I said to Joe J. "If I'd embarrassed me at Killer, I'd be mad at me, too."

Okay, so I was upset enough to throw some shade at Joe J. But not nearly as upset as I would have been if I'd been separated at birth from paper.

DOING THE WRONG THING BY DOING THE RIGHT THING

SOME OF THE MOST SURPRISING WORDS I'VE EVER heard were, "Rebecca Chaikin wants you to ask her to prom." I may as well have won homecoming king again.

I hadn't dated anyone since Colleen Barrett. I hadn't even had a major crush on anyone since Colleen Barrett. I was still attracted to girls, but none had really grabbed my attention in the way they had in the past. Part of that was because I was finally receiving validation in other areas of my life and no longer needed it from one single person. Part of that was because I was maturing, realizing that truly getting along with a woman was more important than whether or not she was the first in my grade to grow boobs. Mostly that second thing.

I was friendly with Rebecca's group of friends. There were five girls in that group. Shayla (the one who told me about Rebecca's desire to go to prom) lived in Forest Hills, so Jacob and I would often see her on the subway. Paulina was one of my copresidents in the improv club. Anya was Ozzie's best friend. And Lilian didn't talk much, which I didn't hold against her because, hey, we've all been there.

Rebecca was my favorite of the group, and we'd been friends for most of our time at Hunter. She was smart and sarcastic but also kind. She was someone who was protective of her people and didn't take any garbage from those outside her circle.

Rebecca was objectively attractive, I knew that. She was one of those girls who starts high school looking like a boy and graduates looking like a boy's fantasy. By senior year, people had caught on, and a lot of people had crushes on Rebecca Chaikin. But in a very unlike me way, I wasn't one of them. I just liked hanging out with her.

When Shayla told me that Rebecca wanted me to ask her to prom, it came out of nowhere, but I was flattered. I took the night to think about it. Going to prom with Rebecca seemed like a great idea. A prom limo with a group of people I liked was appealing, and so was a date I'd enjoy spending the evening with. It certainly beat my original plan, which was no plan at all. I asked Rebecca the next morning, and she said yes and gave me a kiss on the cheek.

Rebecca and I solidified plans that night on the phone. And the closer prom got, the more often we talked. Eventually, our conversations became an everyday thing. We were hanging out in the hall during free periods and eating lunch together and saying goodbye before we went home. It was like we were a couple, except without all of the making out stuff.

It is a strange thing to suddenly realize you're attracted to someone who's already been in your life in another role for such a long time. With Rebecca, it happened one day when she didn't call me back. She had good reason—I found out the next day that her parents were punishing her for coming home late without calling and that they had taken away her phone privileges (something much easier to do back when phones were bolted to the wall). But that night, I was sad. And that's when I realized, "Oh, this is more than a friend now." I realized that I wanted to spend time with her always.

Unfortunately, Rebecca didn't feel the same. I knew that because part of our friendship was her talking to me about the guy she liked. I didn't mind at first since I'd originally put myself in the friend zone. But once I realized I had feelings for Rebecca, I tried to subtly change the conversation whenever dating came up. I wasn't as subtle as I thought I was.

"Rebecca knows you like her," Shayla said, surprising me once more. Shayla definitely had a penchant for gossip. I'd matured enough to know denial of gossip is taken as confirmation, so I simply responded "I know" to take the wind out of Shayla's sails. If Shayla thought that the gossip was no big deal to me, perhaps she wouldn't go around school telling everyone else. My deflection worked, and the rumor died there. But now Rebecca knew, and I knew Rebecca knew. I wondered if this would change our daily routine.

Thankfully, it didn't. Rebecca and I still spent just as much time together and still spent time every day on the phone. That didn't mean that Rebecca liked me, too. But it did mean that Rebecca still enjoyed spending time with me and didn't mind that I liked her. I'd already accepted that she wasn't interested, but I'd have been crushed if it had meant the end of our friendship.

Prom was the first time I'd worn a tuxedo outside of my siblings' weddings. And while my tuxedo was the cheapest one I could find, it still looked way nicer than the hand-me-down T-shirt, twenty-dollar, faded Sears jeans, and baseball hat Rebecca usually saw me wearing.

Prom was fun, as I always enjoyed spending time with Rebecca. We talked and laughed, and we danced to almost every song. Platonic or not, I thought it was wonderful, and Rebecca did, too. Prom was worth all the extra babysitting.

As the last song came on, I asked Rebecca to dance, but she waved me off to talk with Shayla. The group from my limo was sitting around our table exhausted. We knew the merriment was coming to an end, and the rest of the group chose to just survey the room rather than cram one more dance in. It was then that I noticed my homecoming queen, Victoria Layton, sitting by herself at an otherwise empty table.

Victoria and Eugene had broken up two weeks before prom. And rather than go with one of the many latecomers scrambling to ask her out, Victoria went by herself. After a lifetime of being in a couple, it must have felt weird for her to be alone. Especially during the final slow song of the night.

The dance floor was littered with couples, and Victoria sat, just staring at her friends dancing with their dates. And then I saw it—Eugene was dancing with his date, too. Eugene hadn't gone the I-don't-need-anyone-else route that Victoria chose, opting instead for the first cute girl who had showed interest. And Victoria was sitting there, during the last song of prom, watching them dance. The girl who had treated me so kindly all year was sad, and I wanted to do something about it.

I looked around my table. Everyone was happily gabbing away, and Rebecca was riveted by some gossip from Shayla. I thought about my next move. Rebecca had already said no to a dance, and while she was my date, we were not *on* a date. Still, I asked her if she'd mind if I danced with Victoria. Maybe she didn't care. Maybe she didn't hear me correctly. Maybe she thought the question was ridiculous. But Rebecca gave me a quick "go ahead" gesture with her hand and went back to listening to Shayla.

It *was* a ridiculous question, as asking Victoria to dance did not mean we would end up dancing. I may as well have asked Rebecca, "Do you mind if I step away for a moment to pitch for the Mets?"

I stood up and walked over to Victoria's table. "We never did get that dance," I said to a confused look on her face. Victoria probably didn't remember what she had said to me about homecoming. But in the moment, I thought it was smooth.

"What?" Victoria asked. I tried again, but with less subtlety.

"Would you like to dance?"

She said yes, and the two of us proceeded to the dance floor.

Victoria was no longer watching Eugene dance—rather, the reverse was happening. I knew Eugene was watching us dance because everyone was watching us dance. If you polled everyone in Hunter, at any point from the first day of school until that moment, and asked them, "Will Steve Hofstetter and Victoria Layton ever slow dance together?" the answer would have been 100 percent no. Even if Victoria and I were the ones being asked in the poll. Some students would have answered no while watching us dance. They might have assumed it was a hallucination.

My dance with Victoria lasted only a minute or two, as that's how long the second half of a song lasts. But the moment lasted much longer than that. My "debut" at Hunter involved dancing at the junior prom, but that was because I was thrust into a circle against my will. A year later, I'd gained enough confidence to slow dance with someone like Victoria Layton in front of the entire class.

Something comedians need is the ability to not care what people think of them. That's what I'd gained from all those years of improv—knowing that sometimes a scene works and sometimes it doesn't and that whether or not the audience enjoys your choices is often out of your hands. I also learned that it's okay if a scene fails, because you'll get a seemingly infinite amount of other opportunities for success. Life is similar to improv in that way. If Victoria had said no to me, so what? If everyone had laughed at us on the dance floor, so what? If Victoria had said yes, only to douse me with a bucket of pig's blood, okay, that would bother me. But mainly because it's so unoriginal.

I stopped worrying about what people would think of me and just acted. I thought I had a ton of friends in USY, and I was wrong. I thought I was part of a big group at Hunter, and I was wrong. Even Alexa Howard had gotten to know me, appreciated me, and still treated me like garbage. So what did it matter if people liked me or didn't? I wanted to ask Victoria to dance in that moment. So I did, and she said yes, and we danced with hundreds of people watching us. It was fantastic.

After prom, Rebecca's friend Lilian threw a party at her parent's Connecticut house, because that is what rich kids with irresponsible parents do after prom. Most of the senior class went, and it was nice to be part of the limo that had suddenly become the in-crowd. Maybe Lilian, like me, was a quiet kid with a few surprises.

Like I had done with Lindsay Messner at Marley's party three years earlier, I spent most of the party with a girl I was dating but not really dating. Rebecca and I were inseparable at that party, just like we had been for the past few weeks. But things seemed a bit different than they'd been the past few weeks. Things seemed different than they'd been earlier that night.

Rebecca was sitting closer to me, was touching my arm when she laughed at my jokes, and was fixated on everything I was saying. She repeatedly brought up how great it was that I'd asked Victoria to dance. Rebecca talked about how alone Victoria must have felt in that moment and how I not only recognized it but reached out. The thing Rebecca didn't realize is that, had my non-date date expressed anything other than platonic-ism for me, I wouldn't have ever noticed Victoria was at prom, let alone asked her to dance.

Rebecca seemed really touched by my gesture toward Victoria, and she kept touching me. Two hours into the party, Rebecca and I were sitting up against a wall with my arm around her and her leaning on my shoulder. I could have sat like that the entire night.

Rebecca, however, decided she wanted to get another drink. When she tried to stand up, she couldn't. I had the terrible realization that Rebecca's cuddling, her flirtations, and her repetition were being fueled by alcohol. Rebecca, who hadn't ever tried alcohol before that party, was all over me because she was drunk.

I hoped that I was misreading the situation or that the alcohol had just allowed Rebecca to lower her walls. I was terrified that when Rebecca sobered up, she'd forget she'd ever flirted with me, and that our cuddling, like high school, would be over for good. And as all of these thoughts raced through my mind, Rebecca tried to kiss me.

I am sure you are hoping that I did the right thing. That I pulled back. That I didn't take advantage of the situation. That

I didn't let a girl who'd never been drunk before do something she'd regret on prom night.

How long have you been reading this book? Of course I didn't take advantage of Rebecca. Life is not a romantic comedy, and it is also not an after-school special. I simply moved my head to the side and kept talking to Rebecca as if her attempt at a kiss had never happened.

I didn't want to embarrass Rebecca, both for her sake and for mine. If Rebecca felt I'd rejected her, I'd have no chance to actually date her when she was sober. So I pretended like nothing was wrong and hoped her drunk memory would remember things differently than how they had happened. Maybe Rebecca would remember that she wanted to kiss me, but not the actual failed attempt. Maybe not.

The next morning, Rebecca and I took part in a Hunter tradition older than Killer and Carnival and punny mascots. Hunter's prom is always on a Thursday, so after staying up all night, students show up at school on Friday morning still dressed in prom attire. We don't stay for the whole day, as seniors are given that day off. But all the students poke our heads into classes to say hi to our favorite teachers and have breakfast in the cafeteria, and some students even play games of pick-up basketball in full formal wear.

As Rebecca sobered up, she became more and more aloof. I don't know if Rebecca regretted that I stopped her from kissing me or felt embarrassed over the whole incident. But there was something off between us—there was a definite distance. Rebecca and I said our goodbyes as first period started, and I went home to sleep for as long as I could. Despite some after-prom hope, it was clear that Rebecca and I would continue our friendship the way it had been. It was disappointing but not unexpected.

I'd started prom with no shot with Rebecca, and that's how I finished it. Could I have kissed her that night? Absolutely. Would I have been ashamed of myself for the rest of my life for doing so? Also absolutely. Doing the right thing was more important to me than getting the girl.

My dating prospects hadn't changed since the day before, so I didn't have anything to really be sad about. Meanwhile, I got to sit arm in arm with Rebecca for a few hours, and I danced with Victoria Layton. I was sure Shayla was off gossiping about it somewhere.

DOING THE RIGHT THING BY DOING THE WRONG THING

LIKE PROM, IT WAS TRADITIONAL FOR EVERYONE TO STAY up all night after the last day of classes, too. This time, the party wasn't official—just a few of the popular rich kids who somehow rented out a bar despite being only eighteen. It is stunning how often laws get ignored when the lawbreakers have money.

Everyone was invited, even people who didn't usually go to parties. I spent most of the night talking to Rebecca. After a few days, Rebecca had gotten over the embarrassment of our drunken near-kiss, and we resumed our daily phone calls. Thanks to some sleep and thought, Rebecca told me that she really appreciated that I didn't let her make a move, and we grew even closer. At the party, we were inseparable again.

Rebecca and I even left the party together. Not for any

indecent reasons—we were just hungry and talking, and it was four in the morning. So we decided to find a diner and keep the night going. Both Shayla and Randy gave us looks when we said our goodbyes and walked out together. Randy's look was one of *finally*, and Shayla's look was one of *I am so excited for new gossip to tell everyone.*

Rebecca and I discussed those looks at length, as she defended Shayla and I defended Randy. I said Randy was simply rooting for me and Shayla was looking for something juicy. Rebecca said that Shayla was looking out for her and Randy was the one to worry about.

"Let's test the theory," I said.

"How do you plan on doing that?"

"We'll tell each of them different, made-up gossip. See what spreads."

"Excellent plan," Rebecca said. "What do we tell them?"

Before I could come up with an answer, Rebecca suggested we tell Randy and Shayla that we'd hooked up. Considering I wanted that lie to be true, it was hard to argue with it.

We would tell Shayla that my parents were out of town, so we went back to my place and made out. Then we'd tell Randy that Rebecca's parents were out of town so we went back to her place and made out. The real key was that both friends would be sworn to absolute secrecy.

When Rebecca and I finished up at the diner, I had a terrible realization—I didn't have my keys and could not get into my apartment without them. I might be able to get back before my mother left for work if I hurried, but I hated to cut the night short. Even though it was already six A.M.

Rebecca, who lived on what seemed like the opposite side of the world in Brooklyn, volunteered to come back with me to Queens in case I couldn't get in, and then I wouldn't be stranded alone. And that way, we wouldn't have to cut the night short. This was not the kind of thing anyone I'd had a crush on before would have done for me. This was not even the kind of thing that anyone I'd been in a relationship with would have done for me. Did Rebecca have feelings for me, too?

The New York City subway is pretty amazing considering how many people it successfully shuttles back and forth each day. But at six A.M., it is not the most reliable method of conveyance, especially when you're going in the opposite direction of rush hour. Ninety minutes later, Rebecca and I got to my apartment. My mother was already gone.

As much as I wanted to spend the day with Rebecca, we were tired, and I didn't want her to see me as a burden. I had to find a way inside. I remembered my escape plan during Killer. I just had to do it backward.

The living room window was open, so I jumped up and pulled myself onto the outside gate of the window. If I could climb through a ceiling, I could climb through a window. I unlatched the gate, swung out on it, climbed around to the other side, and swung back. I crawled through the window, got a spare key, and joined Rebecca back outside. We got back on the train, as I said there was no way I was sending her all the way to Brooklyn by herself.

Rebecca and I spent most of the ride to Brooklyn leaning against each other sleeping, and I used my years of commuting experience to wake up before her stop. I walked Rebecca to her door, and she gave me a long, lingering hug. At this point in our fourteen-hour revelry, I'd had enough courage to climb a literal wall, but I did not have enough to kiss Rebecca Chaikin. The hug finally ended without me making a move.

"It was a pleasure hooking up with you," Rebecca said. "I'll call Shayla and tell her how it was."

I slept most of the train ride back. The ride wasn't as pleasant as the ride to Rebecca's house—instead of Rebecca, a large, smelly man sat next to me. But I'd still had a wonderful night. I wasn't going to let anyone's stench ruin it.

I passed out for most of the day and then called Randy to fill him in. He didn't ask many questions—just said that he was happy for me. He was so supportive that I felt bad for lying to him. But I had to, if I was going to prove that Shayla's mouth was as big as the guy I sat next to on the subway.

It didn't take long, as Rebecca had already gotten calls from the rest of her group of friends asking about our night at my place. And then I started getting calls from my friends, too. Even Randy called me.

"I thought you said you guys went to her place?" Randy asked.

"But I heard she came to yours?" Shayla had told so many people that even *my* friends heard Rebecca's story instead of mine. Checkmate, Shayla. I filled Randy in on the truth, and his annoyance over being lied to was muted by his appreciation for why. And his pride that he'd passed the test. And his disappointment that it wasn't true.

Randy and Mason also lived in Rebecca's neighborhood in Brooklyn, so the four of us grabbed Chinese food a few days later. When the time came to open our fortune cookies, Rebecca grabbed mine, laughed, and put it in her pocket without letting the rest of us see. I spent a few minutes trying to get her to show me what it said before being distracted by Rebecca's offer for a post-dinner walk along Prospect Park.

Randy and Mason took our walk as their cue to leave, giving Rebecca and I the chance to finally make the rumors come to fruition. And so we walked along Prospect Park, holding hands. Holding hands was a new development, but I did not allow myself to believe that Rebecca's feelings for me had changed. I'd thought I'd lost her friendship once already; the thought of losing it again was too scary. But when it got dark, we went back to Rebecca's house.

The tough part was that Rebecca's mother was home. The easy part was that Rebecca's mom (like everyone's mom except Colleen Barrett's) liked me a lot. Ever since prom, Rebecca's mom had been pestering Rebecca as to why she wasn't dating me. And so, after a bit of small talk in the kitchen, her mother said, "Well, I don't want to get in your way. Why don't you two watch some TV in your room?"

If there was ever a sign that a guy is nonthreatening, it is when a girl's mother encourages him to go to her daughter's room alone with her.

And so, Rebecca and I obliged. But I was still nervous. At this point, my feelings for Rebecca had gone so far beyond crush that I couldn't risk ruining things. Two years earlier, I had convinced myself I was in love with Hope. And yet I had never felt as strongly about anyone as I did about Rebecca.

Unlike my previous crushes, I knew Rebecca really well. Though she was beautiful, my feelings were not based on her looks. Though she made me feel good about myself, my feelings were not based on anything selfish. I felt strongly about Rebecca because I had gotten to know Rebecca.

Rebecca and I didn't watch any TV, but we didn't make out either. We did what we did best and what I liked so much about her. We just talked, and talked, and talked.

Eventually, our conversation made its way to the rumors we'd spread, and I gloated that I was right about Shayla. Rebecca playfully hit me and then apologized by kissing my arm and putting her head on my shoulder. Even then, I still didn't have the courage to kiss her.

What if I had been reading the signs wrong? I'd been wrong about girls in the past. Maybe Rebecca just *really* liked me as a friend.

I know, you want to jump through this book and scream at me. I want to scream at me, too. Of course Rebecca liked me. We were alone, arm in arm, her head on my shoulder, with music playing in her dimly lit bedroom at one A.M. My move was to point all that out.

"You know, we're alone, arm in arm, your head on my shoulder, with music playing in your dimly lit bedroom at one A.M.," I said. "If anyone knew about this, I bet we'd have more rumors spreading."

At that point Rebecca moved away from me. *Oh, damn it.* What if I was right about being wrong? Maybe Rebecca didn't have feelings for me. And now I'd made it awkward.

Rebecca didn't move far. She reached into her pocket, handed me something, and snuggled back into my arms. She had handed me the fortune from dinner, laughing.

"Good luck bestows upon you," it said. "You will get what your heart desires."

I laughed, too. And that is when I kissed her.

I was going away to work at Ramah again that summer, and Rebecca would be going to Rhode Island in the fall. But none of that mattered in the moment. All that mattered was that our first kiss was real, and it was wonderful. I knew that when I refused Rebecca at that party I'd been doing the right thing. That first kiss proved it. And it wasn't until a few weeks later that I learned it was Rebecca who had once called me about the physics homework.

WHEN I SPOKE UP

HUNTER'S SENIOR CLASS WAS GATHERED IN THE AUDI-
torium as it often was—to hear announcements, to discuss important events coming up, and because most of us didn't want to go to class anyway. Once every few weeks, we'd all get to miss a class period to discuss a pressing issue.

Usually the issue was something clerical. The college application process, how to receive advanced placement credits, and other such boring but necessary information for high school seniors. This particular assembly started boring as well—by going over the program for graduation. Suddenly, there was a turn.

"As most of you know, our graduation speech is not given by the valedictorian, but rather by the student whom the class chooses to speak on their behalf."

Most of us did not know that. Hell, I'd been to graduation the year before to support Colleen, and I didn't know that.

The administration went on to tell us that Hunter would be accepting speech submissions over the next two weeks, and my heart soared. I had been speaking in USY for three years, and I could ace this. I actually had a chance to deliver the class speech at graduation. Forget dancing—this would be my real chance to be the person I'd wanted to be.

The administration continued to tell us that we would convene again in the auditorium in a few weeks to hear the top four speeches as selected by the faculty, and the winner of those would be determined by student vote. And my heart sank.

Winning any sort of election at Hunter was not something I ever thought I could do. Unlike USY, I never ran for any offices and never got involved in the leadership of any club where students voted on the leaders. I had been appointed president of the improv club and a teacher had asked me to be coach of the softball team, but I'd never have tried for either if there had been an election. Even when I auditioned for Brick Prison, I never went out for a lead role. Because I knew that I had no shot.

"You should do it anyway," Jacob said. "Who cares if you win or not? Even if you lose the vote, you'll still have given a kickass speech in front of the whole grade."

"What if it sucks?" I asked.

"Write one that doesn't suck," Jacob responded.

Touché.

Over the next two weeks, I wrote and rewrote and rewrote again until I had a speech that didn't suck. I used everything I had learned in history class about speeches with refrains and rallying cries and everything I learned in USY about staying positive and making promises. By the end of those two weeks, I was ready. And I submitted my speech on the last possible day. But not after the deadline—I know what happens when you miss deadlines.

A few days later, I was notified that I was one of the four finalists selected. Getting through the first cut wasn't the part I was worried about. I believed in my speech, and Mrs. Acker was on the selection committee. I knew I could win a popularity contest with Mrs. Acker.

When the senior class convened in the auditorium the following week, I learned that I would be speaking fourth out of four. Damn it. None of the students listening to the speeches particularly wanted to be there, and by the time I was up, they would have sat through three boring speeches that all had similar themes.

The first two speeches were the standard, run-of-the-mill graduation fare. Well written, for sure. But nothing spectacular. We will miss Hunter, we wish you luck next year, we know everyone will be successful, and so on. The speeches were so similar, it was almost cruel to place them back-to-back.

The third speech was a bit . . . different. Micky Ottorino marched onstage with the kind of angry look on his face that scared everyone into paying attention. He also brought his math textbook. We didn't have to spend much time wondering why Micky brought his math textbook—he opened the speech by saying, "Well, we don't need this anymore!" and slammed it to the ground. The rest of the speech was a missive on the sheer amount of time we had all wasted in high school and how worthless the exercise of graduation was. Well, Micky wasn't going to win, though he'd probably get the wouldn't-it-be-hilarious-if vote. The only thing stranger than Micky's speech is that the administration chose it as a finalist. I started to think that only four of us had submitted speeches.

I had to follow that uncomfortable weirdness, so I took a chance.

"Micky," I started, as I picked up his book and walked over to him. "You dropped this."

It got a few laughs, and I began my speech.

"We are leaving," I said. "To where, we are not sure. But we know that we are leaving."

I went on to talk about how uncertain our world was and how much more complex our choices were than our parents' choices.

"Their heroes were Superman, Batman, and Captain America," I said. "In our high school years, all three have died at least once."

My intent was to alternate between the right amount of silly and serious.

"Hunter's advanced academic environment," I continued, "has not taught us just the atomic weight of tungsten and how to say 'where is the nearest hotel?' in Spanish; it has encouraged us to reach out further than the classroom. We have learned how to deal with hunger and AIDS, we have learned how to direct a musical, and we have learned how to throw a fastball."

I took a dramatic pause.

"We have learned how to live," I said. "We have learned how to learn."

I paused again and realized that everyone was quiet. They were listening. The entire senior class was listening to me, actively wanting to hear what I had to say next. This was not a group of students surrounding me in the hallway, rooting for Scarlet Daly to devour me. This was something I'd never experienced before at Hunter—this was respect en masse.

As I got to the finish line, I felt I had them.

"We are headed into what we are told is the real world, and we are not supposed to be ready for it. We are supposed to be afraid and hesitant, we are supposed to be reluctant. So why aren't we?" I asked, again, to silence.

"We've been in the real world for years. We've interacted with those of other cultures; we've held jobs; we've braved subways, busses, and ferries—and all to learn."

They were still silent. Still listening.

There's a line in "New York, New York," that says, "If I can make it there, I'll make it anywhere." This line means that New York is such a tough place to make it that everything else seems easier by comparison. I felt the same about high school. All the garbage I had dealt with from hallway humiliation to principal punishment to ball field bullying had toughened me and given me a voice.

When Tommy Tillet teased me, when Theo Webster threatened me, when Phillip Cuchillo assualted me, I could have been broken. At times, I cracked. I let them embarrass me, scare me, and quiet me. I let them win battles. But I never let them win the war.

I'd always had a problem with the phrase, "You can do anything if you just set your mind to it." It's missing the most important piece of that puzzle. The phrase should be, "You can do anything if you just set your mind to it, surround yourself with the right people, and put the work in."

My right people were everyone from Jacob Corry to Mr. Mikkelsen, from Rebecca Chaikin to Mrs. Acker. My work was everything from improv to softball, from Brick Prison to USY. My years of heartbreak and hope informed that speech. There I was, the quiet kid who once refused to speak in class, holding the attention of every one of my classmates. This was the advice my brother, David, had given me so many years before. This was me risking living my life on the bottom line by reaching for the top.

"We are our own icons," I said, defiantly. "We are ready for the world. We are ready for anything."

I do not know how long the time was in between when I finished and when the crowd applauded, but it seemed painfully long. In reality, it was probably less than a second: the standard, don't-clap-until-we-know-he's-done pause that most crowds will give a speaker. It felt like forever. But their applause was explosive.

"Well," Jacob said as I returned to my seat. "That definitely didn't suck."

And now it was time to see who'd won. The administration explained that if no one got more than two-thirds of the vote, there'd be a run-off between the top two speeches. Waiting for the results the next day was extremely nerve-wracking. I had made the mistake of getting my hopes up, like I'd done in USY. I thought I had a decent chance at this thing. I knew Micky wouldn't win, so the question became whether or not the students wanted the standard graduation fare from the first two speakers or something a little more Freak Hallway.

Like USY, there was no run-off between the first two voters. But unlike USY, I won.

When graduation came, despite having practiced that speech hundreds of times, I had never been as nervous as I was that day. It didn't matter that I knew my speech by heart and that my classmates liked it enough to vote it the winner. I was terrified of screwing up. Graduation was the biggest stage I'd ever been on, and I didn't want to let the opportunity pass.

When the honored alumni guest went off on a weird tangent about the vastness of the universe that made most of the audience confused and uncomfortable, my nerves got even worse. I tried to remind myself that this was just like improv, and if the scene didn't work out, I'd always have another one. My advice to myself didn't work in this particular situation.

"Don't worry, Steve. You can do better at your next high school graduation," wasn't true or comforting.

The alumni speaker finally finished her rant about aliens, and it was my turn.

When you perform, you have one moment to get the audience's attention and set the tone for the rest of the time you're onstage. Like I did when I followed Micky, I had to deal with the uncomfortable weirdness in the room. I had help from one of my heroes.

I was told by Dr. Haanraats I'd have to remove my hat before speaking, so I did. I thought the formality of needing to be hatless was silly, and like everyone else at Hunter, I had learned not to respect authority when it didn't make sense. I took my hat off so it faced the crowd—revealing a Bat-signal that I'd taped to the top of it. The crowd chuckled, I smiled, and I began.

"We are leaving," I began. "To where, we are not sure."

The next few minutes went well, and I was emboldened when the crowd laughed where they were supposed to and applauded where I hoped they would. By the time I reached the critical moment of the speech, I was feeling pretty good about myself.

"We have learned how to live," I said. "We have learned how to learn."

And, like I'd planned, there was a dramatic silence as I dramatically paused. Until a baby very loudly yelled, "Yahhhhhhhhhh!"

Like when Scarlet Daly had confronted me in the hallway, I was given a moment. A pause where everyone's attention was focused on what I was going to say next. I had an opportunity. Unlike that moment in the hallway, I was prepared.

Not the USY snowstorm, not getting into Mr. Mikkelsen's economics class, and not cleaning up after those ferrets—that baby was the most important sliding door of them all. My response to him was simple but set the tone for who I would be the rest of my life.

Improv took over, and without thinking, I turned toward that baby and very seriously said, "Thank you, sir." The room busted up laughing.

From there, the rest of the speech was cake. I held that room in a way I had never held a room before.

"We are ready for the world," I closed. "We are ready for anything."

That time, there was not as much space between my final word and the applause. I smiled, said thank you, and walked back to my seat.

It was over: the speech, high school, and my transformation. All of it was over. I was finally the person I wanted to be.

I was a pretty unhappy teenager. And then I wasn't.

ONE MORE THING

IT WAS MY FIRST WEEK AT COLUMBIA, AND THE PLAN was to go to Times Square and people-watch. As my classmates and I walked through the madness, someone barked at us that they had free tickets to a stand-up comedy show. I'd never seen stand-up live and had always wanted to, so I was immediately drawn in. My new "friends" (people who lived in my dorm) were convinced easily enough, and we headed to the back room of a hamburger joint to watch the "show."

The show turned out to be an amateur night, and many of the acts were terrible. I didn't care—I just loved being in that environment. As we settled our bill, I was talking a mile-a-minute about what I liked and disliked, and I was discussing what I would have done given the chance on stage. On our way out, we thanked the show's MC, who was also working the door. Because it was an amateur night.

"Thanks, Red," she said, extending a flyer. "If you want to come and try it, here's how you sign-up."

My classmates all said, "no, thank you," but I took the flyer.

On the walk to the subway, one of my classmates pressed me.

"*You're* going to do stand-up?"

"Why not?" I asked. "I've done improv before. Seems fun."

"I'd be terrified of the rejection," he replied. "Aren't you afraid of people judging you?"

"No," I laughed. "I went to high school."

I carefully folded the flyer and put it in my wallet so I wouldn't lose it, and I wondered how Rebecca was doing in Rhode Island.

9/8/97

★Whoever said
talk is cheap never
called a 976 number

- Directions on
   shampoo
- who to make fun of, who not
   to make fun of

= Ads during Field of Dreams

- Trying on clothes

- Subway delays

- Comittee of nuts in NYC

- Fashion Cafe (Binge 5.79, Purge 6.95)

- Howard Stern + Janet Reno

- Highschool (No, I was parking cars)

- Parents — too lazy to get divorced

- Hic Jokes (Jim Leyland names)
- Be more Polite... say please before

Everything I Ever Needed to Know
I Learned From Saved By The Bell

by Steve Hofstetter

It's the early 90's, you're sitting in your living room and it's 5:00 pm. You have nothing better to do than to watch television, so you cave in and flip it on. Nowadays, of course, you would turn straight to "The WB," but this scenario takes place ⬚⬚⬚⬚⬚⬚⬚⬚⬚ "Sister Sis-⬚⬚⬚⬚⬚⬚⬚⬚⬚ to the pub-⬚⬚⬚⬚⬚⬚⬚ lip between ⬚⬚⬚⬚⬚ "Jane," on ⬚⬚⬚⬚⬚ nnel Nine. ⬚⬚⬚⬚⬚ hannel-surf ⬚⬚⬚⬚⬚ advertently ⬚⬚⬚⬚⬚ At first you ⬚⬚⬚⬚⬚ n Charge," ⬚⬚⬚⬚⬚ e new fam-⬚⬚⬚⬚⬚ ws such as ⬚⬚⬚⬚⬚ 0" will fill

etcetera.
As the episode s⬚⬚⬚⬚
your skin slowly m⬚⬚⬚⬚
upholstery, you thin⬚⬚⬚⬚

school in Indiana. Remarkably, it quickly became a Southern California High School, in the same building with the same principal and most of the same students.
2) Zack should be in jail. He's committed grand theft auto, kidnapping, forgery, mail fraud, and destruction of public property (to name a few), yet Mr. Belding seems to think detention is the answer. How obviously effective.
3) Family members seem to go in and out of the show for one episode each. Examples of those who have come and gone, never to be seen again: Mr. Belding's hipper, younger brother, Rod.

AND NOW FOR THE

ACKNOWLEDGMENTS

ACKNOWLEDGMENTS

"BETH," WHO NURTURED MY LOVE FOR STORYTELLING and stayed up late with me on summer nights pretending to be sportscasters, actors, directors, and other things I've gotten to be.

"David," who hit baseballs over my head until I was old enough to do the same for him and who lobbed jokes over my head (and continues to do so).

"Leah," who is more like me than I care to admit, and not just because we both have red hair.

My mother, whom I love very much, despite how many times I joke about her in this book, and whom I will be taking out to a very nice dinner sometime soon.

My father, whom I miss very much. Every time I do something that I know he'd have been proud of, I get a little sad knowing I can't show it to him.

Thank you to Russell Best, Jane Dystel, and the entire team over at Abrams/Amulet who worked to publish and design the book. Your tireless creativity is what made this a reality. Without your help, this book would have just been a very long Facebook post.